Fans

"Got it, read it, and liked it, particularly the quote from Pappaw! I think it will become the definitive guide for entrepreneurs and established small business owners alike. It's really packed with information you can use right now, today; I thought it was great. I still want my signed copy!"

—Lisa M.

"I just finished digesting your manuscript. Brother, I have to hand to you…*wow*! That was an entrepreneur's bible. The resources are just overwhelmingly wonderful. I've literally spent hours writing notes and going over certain pages in detail, and I'll continue to use this as a regular research tool. I loved it! Great, great job!"

—Rob C.

"I think Terry Justice is probably the smartest person I know, so everyone should buy his book Dissecting Business when it comes out. You'll learn fun and interesting things about business and life!"

—Alisha S.

Dissecting Business

The Entrepreneur's Guide to Success | Discover what it takes to start and grow your business

TERRY JUSTICE

RBSC Press
PO Box 381
Arley, AL 35541

To purchase more copies or to inquire about Terry, visit www. RealBusinessSolutionCenter.com

ISBN: 1468005588
ISBN-13: 9781468005585

Illustration by Michael Justice

Dissecting Business—The Entrepreneur's Guide to Success: Discover what it takes to start and grow your business / Terry Justice

1. Business 2. Education

Printed in the United States of America by CreateSpace

Contents Page

Acknowledgments   vii
Foreword   ix
Preface   xiii

Chapter 1   Career Direction   1
Chapter 2   Starting a Business   7
Chapter 3   Wise Counsel   15
Chapter 4   Money and Finance   21
Chapter 5   Business Organization   31
Chapter 6   Office Space   41
Chapter 7   Technology   47
Chapter 8   Risk Management   53
Chapter 9   Contracts   55
Chapter 10   Marketing   57
Chapter 11   Selling   83
Chapter 12   Managing Your Bottom Line   93
Chapter 13   Management   97
Chapter 14   Employees   105
Chapter 15   Exit Strategy   107
Chapter 16   Business Plans   111
Chapter 17   Setting Up the Business   143
Chapter 18   Conclusion   147
Bonus Chapter   Biblical Principles of Business   155

Resources   165

Acknowledgments

To all those who have coached me over the years and helped make the Real Business Solution Center a success. To those who have served as mentors, consultants, and friends. I thank you. Without your support and counsel, I would not be the coach I am today.

A heartfelt thank-you to my wife, Melissa, for understanding and supporting my dream! You have listened to me ramble on about business, understood when I worked two jobs, and supported my goals. You sacrificed at home while I built the business. Your help and support are unequaled. You have been my biggest fan throughout my career. There is no way I would be living my dream if it weren't for you.

To Dan Miller, author and coach, I thank you for the support you have provided through *48 Days to the Work You Love*.

To Dave Ramsey, I owe a large thank-you for the inspiration and training I received as a certified financial counselor.

God is the true architect. He knew what direction my life would take and has opened many doors that would have otherwise remained closed. While I never know what is around the corner, I have peace that God's plan for my life is better than I could have imagined.

Foreword

This book should be required reading by everyone who cares about the restoration of America. The very backbone of this great nation is entrepreneurialism. But even if you never intend to own your own business, this book is essential for its potent self-analysis, concise explanation, and straightforward approach to the three critical areas of life. Terry takes his reader step by step through the confusing maze of budget, Bible, and bad decisions as they relate to life and business.

My years in radio, television and media have taught me one thing—those who really succeed do so not because they are good at their trade, but because they understand the basics of business. Take doctors, for example. There are plenty of poor doctors because they spent too much on their education, and then, when turned loose with a license, had no idea how to turn that passion and education into a successful business venture. How do you build your social media? How do you know which aspects of business you will excel, and which you need to hire out? How much money is okay to borrow, or should you save all the money to start your business ahead of time? Where do you go to find the answers to all of this? Sadly, not enough who *do* succeed like to share their secrets of the trade with those who need it the most—people trying to start, save, or sustain a business. If they do, they shroud it all in a hazy fog of mystery, leaving you wondering how on earth they ever "made it" if they can't even tell you what they did! Terry's years in the real world working in hard labor, sometimes more than one job to support his family, combined with his Spiritual foundation, lend them to a "street smarts" approach that is easy to read and refreshing!

Business is complicated, like a human being. You have a skin covering the internal organs, and in some areas, like the brain, you have a hard outer shell that is impossible to see or understand for its complexity. Business is like that, too. Terry's book breaks through that blinding outer cover and exposes business from the inside out with fascinating glimpses into what makes businesses tick that you won't find anywhere else.

I started my own business in 2001. I had no idea where to begin. I knew nothing about business I simply knew I had a skill I wanted to sell. I was (am) a marketer by nature, good enough at predicting trends, and helping communicate a message. I didn't know a thing about business I just wanted to help other businesses be successful by selling their good or service. How on earth was I supposed to learn (or care) about payroll, ledgers, or projections? I spun my wheels for years, and I could have saved time and worry with Terry's book, had it been available to me then. I can honestly say that I wouldn't do it again without a copy of this book in my hand, at all times! Terry has laid out the Cliff Notes and Ten Commandments of business all in one easy, compelling, and even funny read. This book could save you time, money, and gray hair with complete self-analysis, and essential resources for anyone wanting to learn about business, or really take the plunge!

Anyone could start, grow, and sustain a business with the wisdom in *Dissecting Business*. Entrepreneurs like me will be kicking themselves for not having this book with them from the moment they first had the idea to go into business. But Terry Justice delivers the well-organized, simply put and straight forward text so well that you will feel like you paid too little for a book so essential, and packed full of business BAM!

From starting, to building, to social media, to marketing, Terry describes every phase and facet of business so clearly, that you will feel the need to mark it up with highlighters, and keep it with you at all times. This essential tool would make the perfect gift for the graduate, the stay-at-home-mom who dreams big, or the retired business leader who loves his trade. It is a book for anyone who ever celebrated what makes America unique—it is a book for those who love this Country, and want to be a part of restoring her.

I will be honest and say that I had lost my desire for entrepreneurial pursuits with this economy. For the first time in my adult life, I had gone back to work as an employee and frankly, I enjoyed that my boss at Crawford

Broadcasting had to handle the headaches and risk of business ownership that I had decided were a burden. I decided that I liked being on the receiving end of all that goes into owning a business, and probably never would have stopped to think about owning a business again. That is, until I read Terry's book. *Dissecting Business* reminded me about the *story* of business—the poetry and purpose. I had lost my love for business, and felt no sizzle in the word entrepreneur that used to send patriotic chills up my spine. This book made me fall in love with the sexy side of business again, and now I am ready to grab on for the next great adventure!

Dissecting Business is not only your essential, business bible for making a go of entrepreneurialism-- Terry Justice makes you want to grab the flag, sing The Battle Hymn of the Republic, and embrace the American Dream in a whole new way!

 -Gina Loudon, Ph.D.

The Dr. Gina Show

Preface

Have you ever wished there was a simple guide to good business? A *Reader's Digest* version that would help you navigate many of the common pitfalls of business? Well, look no more! This book is intended to be a road map to your business and financial success.

The question many would-be entrepreneurs start with is: "What could possibly be so challenging about setting up a new business?" Anyone should be able to do it, right?

Let me start by telling you a short story about a friend of mine. She and two other friends had gone out for cappuccino on their way shopping. They had placed their orders and were patiently waiting on their coffee. When it arrived they returned to their car and made their way toward the mall.

All at once my friend shrieked, "This is somebody's personal cup. It has his name written on the side."

She immediately called the store manager to express her dissatisfaction with the service. The concerned manager asked, "What name was on the cup?" to which she replied, "Van Capp."

The manager calmly informed her that Van Capp was the abbreviation for the vanilla cappuccino she had ordered. I was on the floor when she told me this story. I can only imagine what the store manager was thinking.

The moral of this story is: You may find that what seems clear initially can be totally different once you gather a little information. Starting a business is no different.

"Shriek – This is someone's personal cup!"

My hope is that this book will provide you with a clear understanding of the many business questions entrepreneurs face.

Anyone can have a great idea, but it takes a lot of effort to run a business. The information in the remaining chapters will provide you with the tools you need to succeed.

First and foremost I want you to understand that you *can't* be the expert in every aspect of your business. Seek counsel from your spouse, friends, other business professionals, pastor, and many others before embarking down the path of business owner.

Remember—the only stupid question is the one you fail to ask!

"A man who wants to lead the orchestra must turn his back on the crowd." —Max Lucado

---

CHAPTER 1

Career Direction

Basics

In this section I will outline the career development process. Whether you are seeking a new career or trying to decide whether self-employment is right for you, the mechanics are the same.

When you begin your career search, there are several questions to ask yourself. The first question should always be "Why do we work?" The answer will vary from person to person, but at the most basic level we work to provide for our family.

This might include:

- Utilities
- Groceries
- Clothes
- Rent/Mortgage
- Car payment
- College
- Vacations
- Shoes (my daughter's personal favorite)

Some people work because they are bored. This is especially true of the baby boomers who have worked all of their lives and retired at a relatively early age.

> *1 Timothy 5:8 tells us that we are to take care of our own, especially those in our own household and if we fail to, we have denied faith and are worse than a nonbeliever.*

If we allow ourselves the luxury of "laying it on the line," we will probably admit we are even happier when we are working. There is a side benefit to working: self-esteem. When we are working, we have a sense of self-worth or a feeling that we are making a contribution to society.

> *"Employment is nature's physician, and is essential to human happiness."*
> *—Galen*

This raises the question: How do we choose a career? Do we choose based on the long-term earning potential? Our abilities? What our friends and relatives think we should do? The answer is no to all of the above. Are you surprised?

You may be very talented in the lawn care field, but if you hate the job, it really doesn't matter how good you are. You will be miserable. You may be a wonderful orator, but if you hate giving speeches, you will never be happy.

The same is true of earning potential. It will never matter how much you make or how strong your abilities are if you are doing something you hate. Ultimately, you will always be miserable. You may even begin to sabotage your own work.

So how *should* we choose a career?

Passion

Webster's Dictionary defines passion as "a strong feeling or emotion, vehement desire, love."

Okay, so you are probably thinking, "passion and career—what an oxymoron!" But what if it could really be that way?

The question we should ask is, "If I could do anything in the world, what would it be?" In other words, "What career will I be passionate about?"

An old philosopher once said, "Choose a job you love and you will never have to work a day in your life." Doesn't that sound *great*?!

In his book *48 Days to the Work You Love*, Dan Miller includes a chart titled "The Wheel of My Life." On the diagram you see the words "How will I be remembered?" I think this speaks volumes about our career choices. Will you be remembered as someone who worked hard, made a lot of money, but never seemed happy? Or will you be remembered as someone who led a balanced life and lived his or her dream?

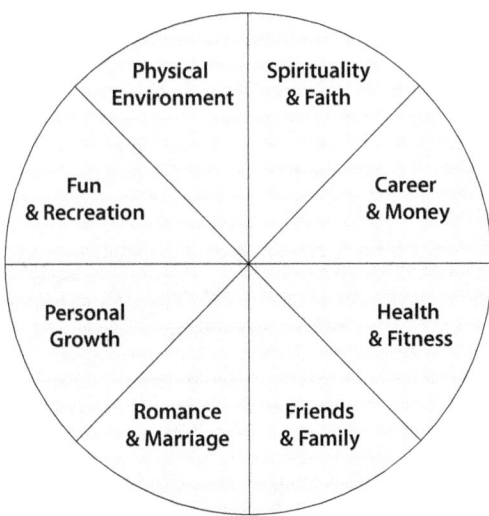

How will you be remembered?

So how do we find our "dream" job?

I think the first step is to ask a few simple questions. Take a moment and write down your answer to the following questions:

What do I love to do more than anything?

_____

_____

_____

_____

If I could do anything, what would it be?

_____

_____

_____

_____

> *"To find out what one is fitted to do, and to secure an*
> *opportunity to do it, is the key to happiness."*
> *—John Dewey*

Personality Profile

Next you should take a few minutes to complete a personality profile. There are many different profiles on the market. The key is to select a profile that provides a list of career choices best suited for your specific personality traits. The personality profile I use in my coaching business can be found at www.realbusinesssolutioncenter.com/profiles-0.

Personality profiles are used to isolate specific characteristics based on a series of scientific questions. The results can be amazing! A good personality profile will not only help you identify your strengths and weaknesses, but it will also help you identify career options that lend themselves to your strengths.

I also recommend that you read Dan Miller's *48 Days to the Work You Love*. Dan provides not only an in-depth look into finding your dream job, but also additional resources, sample cover letters, résumés, and other helpful material.

The real key to choosing a career is to follow your dream. Yes, you need to be realistic and consider the requirements, but at the end of the day, it is up to you to turn your dream into a successful reality.

You can use your personal gifts as a catalyst to starting the business or to land a position with an existing firm. Either way you get to embark on a journey filled with passion.

I use the personality profile with my business coaching clients to help isolate their strengths and weaknesses. This allows us to examine the key resources they need to hire. You may be the best salesperson in the world, but that doesn't mean you should handle the company payroll. Knowing your strengths will quickly become a key asset.

As you read this book, you may decide that being an entrepreneur isn't for you. If that happens, don't worry; there are many great resources to help guide you toward a career you will love. This might include reading books on choosing your career path or engaging a career coach such as my friends Rob Clinton (with 180 Career Coaching) and Joel Boggess (with 4 Points Career Coaching). Find these resources and more at www. RealBusinessSolutionCenter.com/career-development.

Why use a career coach?

If your computer isn't working, you can spend your valuable time trying to identify the problem, or you can find someone who is in the business who can repair the equipment efficiently.

Yes, using a professional will cost you a little money, but why would you struggle with a process that you really don't enjoy? The same is true of coaching. Many business professionals today (myself included) have used coaching services at some point in their careers. Coaching puts you on the fast track to success!

As an additional resource, my company (Real Business Solution Center) provides its members with a career tool called Career Cruising, which is part of the free Member Savings Program. To get started, register at www.realbusinesssolutioncenter.com/jump-start-your-career

The Career Cruising site includes:

- Résumé builders
- Skills assessments
- Career research tools
- Comparative salary information by state
- One of the largest job search engines in the country

If you decide entrepreneurship is right for you, the personality profile will help you isolate your strengths and create a platform that will improve your ability to succeed.

CHAPTER 2

Starting a Business

When starting a business, there are three key building blocks:

1. Passion
2. Planning
3. Value

The first building block is *passion*. As you have already learned, passion is key to the success of any new business.

The second building block is *planning*. I can't say this enough: failing to plan means planning to fail.

Too many times I hear the phrase, "I have this great idea that no one else has ever thought of, and I am going to make millions." All too often we entrepreneurs get ahead of ourselves. We are ready to roll out new products before we understand the implications.

Sound familiar?

As difficult as this concept may sound, you *cannot* let your vision get ahead of planning. I will cover business plans in greater detail in another chapter, but for now let it suffice to say, you can't start a successful business without proper planning.

The third building block is *value*. Passion and planning are essential to any successful business, but without value they too will struggle.

Webster's Dictionary defines value as "worth, importance, to esteem, to regard."

What value will your company bring to the market? How will you create esteem and high regard for your company?

By now you should have a good idea of where your passion lies and realize how important it is to establish a plan and value for your business.

So where do we begin? Let's start by defining the value your company will offer.

Take a few minutes to create a detailed value proposition that describes, specifically, who your customers will be, your competitors, what makes your company different/unique, your key success factors, and how you plan to make money. Answering these questions will help clarify your vision and save you time later on.

_____

_____

_____

_____

_____

_____

_____

_____

_____

_____

_____

_____

_____

_____

_____

Review the value proposition you have created. What makes yours unique?

_____

_____

_____

_____

_____

Now ask yourself the following question: "If I were to hand this piece of paper to one of my competitors, could that person say the same thing about his or her company?"

If the answer is yes, then you aren't adding value and that will force you to compete on price. Complete this exercise until you have a truly unique value that sets you apart.

Foundational Planning

Now we will begin to form a foundational plan for your business.

All too often, people think they can start a business today and make big money tomorrow. I call this the "Field of Dreams" mentality (if you build it, they will come). It simply isn't so! It takes time to build a business unless you have some unusual skill set, product, or service.

TIP: STARTING YOUR OWN BUSINESS IS OFTEN THE BEGINNING TO LEARNING MORE ABOUT YOURSELF.

You must also know when to quit. Entrepreneurs must employ the power of positive quitting. Most of us view quitting as something negative, but it's not. From a very early age, we are taught that winners never quit and quitters never win. In reality, winners quit all the time. They make conscious and strategic decisions to discontinue tasks that aren't creating the results they desire.

This is exactly why professional athletes hire personal trainers and spend hours on the practice field. Where would Tiger Woods or Phil Mickelson be without all of the trainers and coaches they have used throughout their careers? Where would Barry Bonds or Alex Rodriguez be without all of the hours spent practicing in the batting cage?

When you quit all the things that aren't working for you, and when you stop tolerating the negative things that hold you back, you create a positive flow in your business.

As a business coach, I often recommend business owners review how they are spending their time. If they are spending significant time on an activity that could have been done at a lower cost by someone else, they should consider outsourcing it.

A prime example is the payroll function. The key is to avoid the trap of doing everything yourself. Guard your time and save it for activities that will enable you to strengthen and grow your business.

Business Plans

Before you start a new career or open a new business, you need a well-thought-out business plan!

As coaches we preach passion, but all the passion in the world can't overcome a poorly thought-out business concept. As you begin to lay out the plans for your new venture, you should focus on your core expertise. Identify your weakest areas and the resources you will employ to manage those aspects of the business.

> *"For which of you, intending to build a tower, does not sit down first and count the cost, whether he has enough to finish it—lest, after he has laid the foundation, and is not able to finish, all who see it begin to mock him, saying 'This man began to build and was not able to finish'?"*
> *(Luke 14:28–30)*

Would you expect your general contractor to begin construction on your new home without a blueprint? Absolutely not. Right? Well, the same holds true for a new business. Planning is essential to success. Make this your new business mantra: failing to plan means planning to fail.

Here are six simple rules to starting a business:

- Undercapitalization is arguably the number one reason for business failure. In light of the current economy, which can reoccur at any time in the future, it is imperative for any small business to minimize not only its expenses but also its debt and loan payments. Low debt ratios can also increase your ability to obtain additional funding should the need arise. We will talk about business loans in greater detail in a later chapter.

- Make a business plan, review the plan, rewrite the plan, and revisit your plan as often as you can—monthly, quarterly, or at the very least annually.

- Implement strong back-office policies. Everything runs better when the players know the rules. Look at any organized sport.

- Maintain a close watch on your receivables. Don't ever let past-due balances go for more than sixty to ninety days. The longer you wait, the less likely you will collect.

- Preserve your bottom line at all cost. No amount of marketing, coaching, or business technique will save your business if you don't have money coming in.

- Write down where you spend your time. That way you can revisit what you've done to see if you're spending too much time (or not enough) in any one area of your business, and make adjustments as necessary. If you find yourself spending too much time on administrative duties in lieu of core business functions, identify an additional resource.

TIP: THIS DOES NOT MEAN YOU SHOULD TAKE THE PATH OF LEAST RESISTANCE BY HIRING FAMILY!

Family can offer an economical and convenient solution, but you *must* ensure they possess the skill and passion to do the job!

Far too many business owners try to do everything. Unfortunately, when they venture out of their area of expertise, the business suffers.

Remember, it takes time to build a business unless you have some unusual skill set, product, or service. Even then, be cautious as you move forward.

Every business venture is different, but as a general rule, I offer the following key recommendations:

- Know the cost of the venture before you begin.

- Have a well-laid-out business plan that you revisit often.
- Surround yourself with people who are knowledgeable in areas that you aren't.
- Before you start seek advice from a knowledgeable business coach.
- Don't go into debt if at all possible and minimize debt when it is necessary.

All too often I see clients who have a fantastic skill set in their chosen profession, but they really aren't prepared to run a company. This is why it is so important for them to surround themselves with people who are knowledgeable in other areas (accounts payable, contracting, payroll, marketing, etc.).

Once a business owner has the basics in place, he or she can hang on and enjoy the ride!

> *"By working faithfully eight hours a day you may*
> *eventually get to be a boss and work twelve hours a day."*
> *—Robert Frost*

CHAPTER 3

Wise Counsel

Using a qualified counselor can mean the difference between a profitable and a failed business.

> *"Plans fail for lack of counsel, but with many advisers they succeed." Proverbs 15:22*

Remember, information is worthless until it is analyzed and applied properly; then it becomes powerful knowledge and a competitive advantage. Unless guided with relevant one-on-one action plans, start-ups will likely fail, give up in frustration, or miss opportunities.

There are a host of resources available to help you reach your goals. I will highlight some of the more widely used resources below.

One-on-One Business Coaching

Nothing beats one-on-one business coaching. Many successful entrepreneurs (myself included) have received business coaching at one time or another. If you are struggling with payroll, you should call in a business coach specializing in payroll activities. Likewise, if you need help with your contracting and purchasing activities, you should call in an expert in that field. A personal business coach can help you create business plans, establish goals, and sort through volumes of data in a short amount of time. One-on-one business coaching is typically fee based, but you will find no better investment for your time or business.

As a business coach, I help clients get their ideas off the ground. With our assistance they become profitable much faster than they would have on their own. Hiring me saves them time in trying to figure out the best strategies so their money isn't wasted on marketing or systems that won't add value to their bottom line.

Business coaches help people get from where they are to where they want to be by focusing on three primary areas:

- What's working?
- What's not working?
- What's next?

The answer to these three simple questions can help you get started on the road to success.

Coaching Organizations and Centers

Are there any free coaching resources? Yes!

While you do not receive the advantage of a dedicated one-on-one business coach, there are a host of free services in the market. Find many examples listed on the resources page at www.RealBusinessSolutionCenter. com/resource-center, including:

Small Business Administration (SBA)—You will find a host of online resources and self-help manuals on the SBA website, www.sba.gov.

SCORE Counseling—SCORE is a national association dedicated to helping small business owners form and grow their businesses. At the time of this writing, SCORE has 364° chapters in the United States as well as in U.S territories, and they are partners with the U.S. Small Business Administration (SBA). SCORE offers free coaching from experts in the community. To find a SCORE counselor in your area, visit www.score.org.

Small Business Development Centers (SBDCs)—The Small Business Development Center network is an interinstitutional program to enhance economic growth by providing management and technical assistance to small businesses. Certified business counselors are available in Small Business Development Centers located across the United States.

Procurement Technical Assistance Centers (PTACs)—Congress created the Procurement Technical Assistance Program (PTAP) to help businesses seeking to compete successfully in federal, state, and local government contracting opportunities. Funded through cooperative agreements between the Department of Defense (DoD) and state/local entities, ninety-four of its centers provide a range of expert services at little or no charge.

Women's Business Centers (WBCs)—Women's Business Centers represent a national network of nearly one hundred educational centers designed to assist women start and grow small businesses. WBCs operate with the mission to "level the playing field" for women entrepreneurs who still face unique obstacles in the world of business. Through a management of technical assistance provided by the WBCs, entrepreneurs, especially women who are economically or socially disadvantaged, are offered comprehensive training and counseling on a vast array of topics in many languages to help them start and grow their own business.

Chamber of Commerce—Every large city has a Chamber of Commerce. This can be a valuable resource for a new business. Most offer a low membership fee for small businesses. Typical Chamber benefits include:

- Free meeting rooms (by appointment)
- Information on new businesses moving into the community
- Mailing lists
- Low-cost advertising in community events
- Opportunities to speak to other business groups
- Networking events

National Minority Supplier Development Council (NMSDC)—The National Minority Supplier Development Council provides a direct link between corporate America and the minority-owned business community. NMSDC is one of the country's leading business membership organizations.

Minority Business Enterprise Center (MBEC)—This is a program of the Department of Commerce's Minority Business Development Agency. MBEC employs a comprehensive strategy that includes a nationwide network of business assistance resources.

Entrepreneurial Centers—Many cities offer entrepreneurial business options, also known as an Innovation Depot or incubator program. Centers like these typically provide access to office space, venture capital, and other specialized resources.

The most well-developed centers offer:

- Services for a start-up which could include space

- Free resources for the small business community (from SCORE and others)

- Resources to promote supplier diversity (including HUBZone, veteran, service-disabled veteran, sheltered workshops, etc.)

- Fee-based services provided by various business consultants (specialized education, one-on-one consulting, etc.)

- Funding resources

- Workshops on specific topics (state bid laws, how to complete a formal RFP, etc.)

- Access to specialized resources for patent assistance, reading blueprints/takeoffs, payroll, etc.

- Start-up resources (developing a business plan, obtaining business licenses, etc.)

- Meeting rooms

Some even offer a coffee-shop atmosphere where you can bring your laptop and conduct business on-site.

One such resource is the online business community at www.RealBusiness SolutionCenter.com, where you will find access to:

- Personal coaching
- Regional resources
- Workshops
- Collaborative forum
- Career resources
- Member savings programs
- Capital resources
- Bid bulletin boards
- Supplier database
- And much more

Other great examples include:

The Disney Entrepreneur Center—The Disney Entrepreneur Center provides a single location where small businesses can access a variety of business resources, technology, research tools, and more than eight resident support organizations.

The Birmingham Business Resource Center—This center provides a "one-stop stop" for small business development. The goal of the center is to: assist the City of Birmingham's economic development efforts; promote and assist the growth of small businesses by providing programs that help access needed capital; benefit the community by fostering increased employment opportunities through the expansion of business, industry, and economic development; and provide a convenient location for people seeking assistance in establishing, growing, or expanding small business enterprises. Learn more at www.bbrc.biz.

Genesis Center—The Genesis Center is a support network developed to help Newfoundland and Labrador knowledge-based businesses/entrepreneurs create high-growth enterprises. It provides a wide range of resources and services for its clients with a long-term goal of preparing its clients to become "investor ready." There is a competitive application process, but its success rate of "graduate" businesses is very impressive. Businesses grow here for several years before launching on their own—but by that time, they've ironed out the wrinkles and have been in business for that critical start-up period. Learn more at www.genesis.mun.ca/GenesisCentre.

Innovation Depot—Innovation Depot is a business incubation facility and program that focuses on the development of emerging biotechnology/life science, information technology, and service businesses.

Innovation Depot combines the expertise of business incubation professionals with a next-generation facility offering businesses the space and equipment they need to take a business from concept to reality. The 140,000-square-foot facility offers companies the room they need to start and grow, including flexible floor plans and shared conference rooms.

Other features include ample and free on-site parking, full janitorial services, twenty-four-hour security, an on-site restaurant/catering service, and tenant-only private green space. Learn more at www.innovationdepot.net.

Seeking wise counsel before you start will help to uncover issues you might otherwise miss!

CHAPTER 4

Money and Finance

What comes next? Money!

Undercapitalization is arguably the number one reason for business failure. As a business coach, I often have clients tell me they want to start their own business but lack the capital (they have no money). I believe there is a great advantage in that line of thinking.

The advantage comes not because you need money to start a business. Instead, it is that you *recognize* that it takes money to start a business before you begin the process. Recognizing the need is half the battle. Far too many entrepreneurs enter into the business world believing the money will magically appear. Trust me, there is no pot of gold waiting at the end of the rainbow!

"I know what I want to do, but I just don't have the money to make it happen." Have you ever felt that way?

Well, you are not alone. Most small business owners feel the same way. The question of money is without a doubt the most difficult to answer.

It will likely take twice as long as you think to generate the cash flow you desire for your business. Your business cash flow has to be sufficient to cover not only your daily business expense but your personal salary requirements as well.

TIP: *NEVER* UNDER ANY CIRCUMSTANCES SHOULD YOU TAKE OUT A LOAN TO COVER YOUR PERSONAL SALARY AND EXPENSES!

Without a strategy to handle this situation, your enterprise is destined to failure. Everything related to start-up is critical; however, cash is at the center.

The questions I encounter most regarding money are:

- Should I take out a personal loan to start my business?
- Should I try to get a Small Business Administration (SBA) loan?
- Do I need to have cash in the bank before I start my business?
- Should I seek out venture capital to start my business?

The short answer is to never assume additional debt unless it is absolutely necessary.

So, how do you get started?

We will address these questions and more in the coming sections. First let's focus on the basics of business finance.

> *"Money isn't the most important thing in life, but it's reasonably close to oxygen on the 'gotta have it' scale."*
> *—Zig Ziglar*

Banking

Your business accounts should *always* remain separate from your personal accounts. If your company needs a cash injection, you should make a transfer from your personal account into the business account. All business expenses should be paid from the business account even if it means transferring money.

Each account (business and personal) should be set up with an established budget. But how can you establish a budget if you haven't started the business? Your initial budget should include a realistic estimate (your best educated guess). Once you go live, you can always make adjustments.

I recommend using Quicken to establish budgets and download banking transactions; however, the same can be accomplished by using one of the

Excel budgeting forms at www.RealBusinessSolutionCenter.com/resource-center/financial-resources or the simple budget worksheets in the back of this book.

Depending on the structure of your business, you might also consider using QuickBooks or Peachtree to manage your banking and other business transactions.

Business Loans

Most businesses can be started with relatively little cash. You can start with a part-time/side business while working a full-time job. Drop ship inventory from the warehouse. Process orders after hours (nights and weekends).

I have found that many businesses can be started with as little as $5,000 in the bank. In fact, I started my business with only $100 in the company bank account. There are of course many businesses (including a franchise) that require significant investments in space, inventory, personnel, and other up-front expenses.

There are many factors to consider; however, I do not recommend taking out a loan to start your business. It is far better in the long run to have the money on hand or cash flow the business (pay as you go).

If you assume a personal loan for your business, you become personally liable for the balance due.

While this may seem appropriate at first glance, you may be placing your family at risk. What happens if the business doesn't take off as expected? You still have a bank loan that has to be paid. That likely means you have to take cash out of your personal account to cover the balance. If so, then you are removing cash that has been set aside to take care of your family needs.

If you *must* take out a loan, make sure it is no greater than the amount of money you have in your personal savings account. While the risks are still there, your savings account can cover the loss without placing your family at risk.

Never under any circumstances should you take equity out of your home or place your home as collateral to start your business. I have seen too many business owners step out on that limb only to lose their home when the business fell on hard times.

Again, your *primary* responsibility is to take care of your family.

Every business has ups and downs. As such, it is very common for business owners to find that their cash flow is limited—perhaps because they have just taken on additional business or perhaps due to a decline in sales.

When this occurs there are a few simple lending options that may help you survive the short-term cash flow shortage without placing your family at risk. There are programs specifically designed to assist small business owners frustrated by a shortage of working capital required to run their business.

These lending options include:

- Contract financing
- Accounts receivable financing
- Purchase order financing
- Equipment financing

There are companies in the market that will provide short-term loans using a purchase order, contract, or outstanding receivable as collateral. If you have just been awarded a new contract and you lack the capital to purchase the necessary materials, you could consider a short-term loan using the contract as collateral. You get the cash up front and repay (with interest) when you receive payment from your customer.

If you find that a capital loan is absolutely necessary, there are a number of resources available, including SBA, Foundation Capital, Wallace Capital Funding, and Seedco.

Find a more comprehensive list at www.RealBusinessSolutionCenter.com/financing-and-capital-funding/funding-sources.

Here are a few key considerations when determining how much start-up funding is required:

- Cost of sales
- Cost of inventory
- Distribution costs
- Professional fees
- Technology costs
- Administrative costs
- Sales and marketing costs
- Wages and benefits

Some of the more widely used methods for acquiring capital include:

- *Save up* (the best option; self-financing from the founder's cash assets)
- Commercial loan from a bank or other lender
- SBA loan
- Lease financing
- Venture capital from private investors
- Financing from strategic partners
- Financing from potential customers

Venture Capital

There is no need to further define the traditional lending process in this book; however, I would like to leave you with additional insight into the venture capital arena.

Many entrepreneurs think of venture capital as free money. In reality, venture capital can carry significant requirements.

General parameters for venture capital include:

- Borrower must have "skin in the game" (you must assume some of the risk).
- Venture capital lenders often require a 20 to 30 percent return.

- Venture capital lenders may require a 20 to 30 percent equity position in your company.

- Venture capital lenders typically expect to be made whole on VC money in twenty-four to thirty-six months.

- Most require a formal business plan with a credible pro forma.

- They will want to know the name of your CPA, banker, partners, etc.

- They will expect to see a formal business plan before consideration.

Venture capital investors are also called angel investors. They can provide tremendous value, but before you move forward with a venture capital arrangement, you *must* know the parameters and what the impact will be on your business. In certain instances you could be giving up rights and control to a major portion of your company when you enter into a venture capital arrangement.

When entering into a venture capital arrangement, know the rules!

Borrowing and lending have been a part of life from the beginning of time. Today we have a very complex monetary system. We have mortgages, auto loans, credit cards, personal loans, lines of equity, and many other forms of lending. Companies borrow large sums of money with the intent of making payments over an extended period. This practice has contributed to too many people borrowing well beyond their means to repay debts.

Financial pressures from debt have led to bankruptcy, divorce, illegal activity, and worse. There are inherent dangers involved with borrowing money. Know the rules and risks before you embark down that path.

> *"Do not withhold good from those to whom it is due, when it is in your power to do it. Do not say to your neighbor, Go and come back, and tomorrow I will give it."*
> *(Proverbs 3:27–28)*

If it appears that the loan will place your personal assets or family at risk, you should walk away from the opportunity.

Savings/Emergency Fund

I recommend a savings balance of at least three times (preferably six times) your normal monthly business expenses. Notice I said *business expenses.*

As I stated earlier, your personal and business finances should always remain separate. That means you should have two budgets, two emergency funds, two of everything. If for example, you have saved up enough money to cover six months' worth of personal expenses, but nothing for the business, then you are not ready to pursue a new business opportunity.

You are probably asking yourself, "Once I have been in business for a few months, it will be easy to calculate the appropriate value, but how do I start?"

Conduct an inventory of anticipated monthly expenses (payroll, cell phone, utilities, inventory, rent, shipping, vehicles, technology, etc.). Don't worry about having an exact number to start. This exercise is merely to give you a reasonable starting value for your company's savings account and budget.

You should revisit this number after you have been in business for a few months. Your savings allocations should be adjusted at least once annually to coincide with business growth and expense.

Having three to six months' worth of expenses in your company savings account will also help you stave off any short downturn in the economy. (Just make sure to put it back if you have to use it.)

You can use the RBSC Quickie Budget for business in the back of this book to get you started. Find a more comprehensive list of financial resources at www. RealBusinessSolutionCenter.com/resource-center/financial-resources.

Your savings account should never be treated as anything more than insurance. It is intended to cover the unforeseeable emergency. Your savings should never be placed in a long-term interest-bearing account such as an investment. The key is liquidity of the cash. When you need it, you need to get to it fast and without penalty.

I recommend a money market account with check-writing privileges.

When it comes to financing your new business venture, the most important advice I can give is:

- Always protect the basic needs of your family!

- Never assume loans, credit cards, or use personal cash reserves to the point of jeopardizing the financial interests of your family. Ensure you have a plan that will at a minimum allow you to provide food, shelter, clothing, and transportation for your family even if the business venture were to fail.

- If you are leaving a full-time position, make sure you have at least a six-month personal emergency fund to replace your current salary while the business grows.

TIP: CREDIT CARDS AND FICO SCORES DIDN'T EXIST PRIOR TO THE 1970S.

Financial Baby Steps for Business

Step 1—$1,000 business emergency fund

Step 2—Pay off all business debt (excluding your building)

Step 3—Have three to six months' worth of business operating expenses in savings

Step 4—Reinvest 15 percent of your business profits into the company

Step 5—Pay off building loans

Step 6—Invest in your employees

Step 7—Donate to charity

---

*"Almost any man knows how to make money, but not one
in a million knows how to spend it."*
—Henry David Thoreau

CHAPTER 5

Business Organization

Now it is time to think about business ownership. Should you set up your business as a sole proprietorship? LLC? S corp? Inc.?

This is a basic question that all business owners must ask. But which one is right for you?

As you would expect, there are advantages and disadvantages to each. In this next session I will outline the differences.

When you open a new business, you must decide what form of business entity to establish. The form of business ownership you choose determines the amount of regulatory paperwork you are required to file, the personal liability you will assume, and the taxes you are required to pay.

The following provides a brief summary of the most common business structures:

- Sole Proprietorship—A business owned and managed by one individual who is personally liable for all business debts and obligations.

- Limited Liability Company (LLC)—A hybrid legal structure that provides the limited liability features of a corporation and the tax efficiencies and operational flexibility of a partnership.

- S Corporation—A special type of corporation created through a tax election. An eligible domestic corporation can avoid double taxation (once to the shareholders and again to the corporation) by electing to be treated as an S corporation.

- Corporation—A legal entity owned by shareholders.

- Partnership—A single business owned by two or more people.

- Nonprofit—An organization engaged in activities of public or private interest where making a profit is not a primary mission. Some nonprofits are exempt from paying federal taxes.

- Cooperative—A business or organization owned by and operated for the benefit of those using its services. A cooperative is not a legal structure.

The next few pages will provide a more comprehensive description of each classification. I have used the Wikipedia definition as the basis. Don't worry if this section is too technical; it is intended merely as a reference. I have included additional information on the Sole Proprietorship and LLC structures because they are the most common for start-up businesses.

Sole Proprietorship—from Wikipedia—A sole proprietorship, also known as a sole trader, or simply proprietorship, is a type of business entity that is owned and run by one individual and where there is no legal distinction between the owner and the business. All profits and all losses accrue to the owner (subject to taxation). All assets of the business are owned by the proprietor, all debts of the business are the owner's debts, and the owner must pay them from personal resources. This means the owner has unlimited liability. It is a "sole" proprietorship in the sense that the owner has no partners (partnership).

Sole proprietorships are relatively easy to start up. There are fewer regulations, and the owner has the full discretion to make decisions. Likewise, the owner gets to take all of the profits.

As a sole proprietor you are required to pay self employment tax, however the most significant disadvantage is the personal risk. As a sole proprietor there is no separation from business and personal liability.

Many entrepreneurs start their businesses out as sole proprietorships even if they later decide to change to an LLC or some other organizational structure.

If your business model has little or no risk then Sole Proprietorship may be a good option to consider.

LLC (Limited Liability Company)— From Wikipedia: A limited liability company or a company with limited liability (abbreviated L.L.C. or LLC or W.L.L.) in the law of the vast majority of United States jurisdictions is a legal form of business company that provides limited liability to its owners. Often incorrectly called a "limited liability corporation" (instead of *company*), it is a hybrid business entity having certain characteristics of both a corporation and a partnership or sole proprietorship (depending on how many owners there are). An LLC, although a business entity, is a type of unincorporated association and is not a corporation. The primary characteristic an LLC shares with a corporation is limited liability, and the primary characteristic it shares with a partnership is the availability of pass-through income taxation. It is often more flexible than a corporation and it is well suited for companies with a single owner.

The key advantage to forming an LLC is the separation of personal and business liability. If your business will have risk then you may want to consider setting up an LLC to help protect yourself from personal liability.

 It is important to understand that limited liability does not imply owners are always fully protected from personal liabilities. Courts can and do pierce the corporate veil of LLCs when some type of fraud or misrepresentation is involved, or under certain situations where the owner uses the company as an "alter ego."

An LLC can have one or more members. When you create an LLC the members of the LLC become the owners.

In most states LLCs are managed by their members in proportion to their membership interests. (The percentage of the business they own) In some states such as Georgia, however, each member has an equal right to participate in the management of the LLC unless there is a specific provision in the articles of organization or operating agreement to the contrary. This is why it is imperative that you seek out a qualified CPA to assist you through the process. LLCs must also file a document to form the LLC with the secretary of state (or other specified governmental office) of the state where the persons who form the LLC choose to organize it. This document is usually referred to as "Articles of Organization" or "Certificate of Organization," depending on the state.

For U.S. federal income tax purposes, when an LLC has only one member, it is treated as a "disregarded entity and the owner reports the LLC's income on his or her own tax return on Schedule C.

Some of the more notable advantages, as noted on Wikipedia, are:

- An LLC can elect to be taxed as a sole proprietor, partnership, S corporation, or C corporation (as long as it would otherwise qualify for such tax treatment), providing much flexibility.

- There is limited liability, meaning that the owners of the LLC, called "members," are protected from some or all liability for acts and debts of the LLC depending on state shield laws.

- There is much less administrative paperwork and record keeping than a corporation.

- There is pass-through taxation (i.e., no double taxation), unless the LLC elects to be taxed as a C corporation.

- Using default tax classification, profits are taxed personally at the member level, not at the LLC level.

- LLCs in most states are treated as entities separate from their members, whereas in other jurisdictions case law has developed deciding LLCs are not considered to have separate legal standing from their members LLCs in some states can be set up with just one natural person involved.

- Membership interests of LLCs can be assigned, and the economic benefits of those interests can be separated and assigned, providing the assignee with the economic benefits of distributions of profits/losses (like a partnership), without transferring the title to the membership interest

Unless the LLC has chosen to be taxed as a corporation, income of the LLC generally retains its character, for instance as capital gains or as foreign sourced income, in the hands of the members.

Disadvantages include:

- Although there is no statutory requirement for an operating agreement in most states, members of a multiple member LLC who operate without one may run into problems as, unlike state laws regarding stock corporations, which are very well developed and provide for a variety of governance and protective provisions for the corporation and its shareholders, most states do not dictate the governance and protective provisions for the members of a limited liability company. Thus, in the absence of such statutory provisions, the members of an LLC can only establish governance and protective provisions pursuant to contract, in the form of an operating agreement.

- It may be more difficult to raise financial capital for an LLC as investors may be more comfortable investing funds in the better-understood corporate form with a view toward an eventual IPO. One possible solution may be to form a new corporation and merge into it, dissolving the LLC and converting into a corporation.

- Many states, including Alabama, California, Kentucky, New York, Pennsylvania, and Tennessee, levy a franchise tax or capital values tax on LLCs. In essence, this franchise or business privilege tax is the "fee" the LLC pays the state for the benefit of limited liability. The franchise tax can be an amount based on revenue, an amount based on profits, or an amount based on the number of owners or the amount of capital employed in the state, or some combination of those factors, or simply a flat fee, as in Delaware. In 2007, Texas replaced its franchise tax with a "margin tax." This is paid as: tax payable equals revenues minus some expenses with an apportionment factor. In most states, however, the fee is nominal, and only a handful charge a tax comparable to the tax imposed on corporations.

- The District of Columbia considers LLCs to be taxable entities, thus eliminating the benefit of flow-through taxes by subjecting members to double taxation.

- Renewal fees may also be higher. Maryland, for example, charges a stock or nonstock corporation $120 for the initial charter and $100 for an LLC. The fee for filing the annual report the following year is $300 for stock corporations and LLC, and zero for nonstock corporations. In addition, certain states, such as New York, impose a publication requirement upon formation of the LLC, which requires that the members of the LLC publish a notice in newspapers in the geographic region that the LLC will be located that it is being formed. For LLCs located in major metropolitan areas (e.g., New York City), the cost of publication can be significant.

- Some creditors will require members of up-and-starting LLCs to personally guarantee the LLC's loans, thus making the members personally liable for the debt of the LLC.

- The management structure of an LLC may be unfamiliar to many. Unlike corporations, they are not required to have a board of directors or officers.

- Taxing jurisdictions outside the United States are likely to treat a U.S. LLC as a corporation, regardless of its treatment for U.S. tax purposes, for example if a U.S. LLC does business outside the United States or a resident of a foreign jurisdiction is a member of a U.S. LLC.

- The LLC form of organization is relatively new, and as such, some states do not fully treat LLCs in the same manner as corporations for liability purposes, instead treating them more as a disregarded entity, meaning an individual operating a business as an LLC may in such a case be treated as operating it as a sole proprietorship, or a group operating as an LLC may be treated as a general partnership, which defeats the purpose of establishing an LLC in the first place, to have limited liability (a sole proprietor has unlimited liability for the business; in the case of a partnership, the partners have joint and several liability, meaning any and all of the partners can be held liable for the business's debts no matter how small their investment or percentage of ownership is).

- The principals of LLCs use many different titles—e.g., member, manager, managing member, managing director, chief executive officer, president, and partner. As such, it can be difficult to determine who actually has the authority to enter into a contract on the LLC's behalf.

C Corporation, or Inc.—from Wikipedia—A C corporation (or C corp.) is a corporation in the United States that, for federal income tax purposes, is taxed under 26 U.S.C. § 11 and Subchapter C (26 U.S.C. § 301 et seq.) of Chapter 1 of the Internal Revenue Code. Most major companies (and many smaller companies) are treated as C corporations for federal income tax purposes. A corporation *must* file under Subchapter C if it fails to meet even one requirement to qualify as an S corporation.

The income of a C corporation is taxed, whereas the income of an S corporation (with a few exceptions) is not taxed under the federal income tax laws. The income, or loss, is applied, pro rata, to each shareholder and appears on his or her tax return as Schedule E income/(loss).

Steps to Forming a C Corporation

According to Nolo, a prospective creator of a C corporation must:

- Choose an available business name that complies with his or her state's corporation rules.

- Appoint the initial directors of the corporation.

- File formal paperwork, usually called articles of incorporation, and pay a filing fee that ranges from $100 to $800, depending on the state where he or she incorporates.

- Create corporate bylaws, which lay out the operating rules for the corporation.

- Hold the first meeting of the board of directors.

- Issue stock certificates to the initial owners (shareholders) of the corporation.

- Obtain licenses and permits that may be required for his or her business.

S Corporation—from Wikipedia—An S corporation, for U.S. federal income tax purposes, is a corporation that makes a valid election to be taxed under Subchapter S of Chapter 1 of the Internal Revenue Code.

In general, S corporations do not pay any income taxes. Instead, the corporation's income or losses are divided among and passed through to its shareholders. The shareholders must then report the income or loss on their own individual income tax returns.

Like a C corporation, an S corporation is generally a corporation under the law of the state in which the entity is organized. S corporations are separate legal entities from their shareholders and, under state laws, generally provide their shareholders with the same liability protection afforded to the shareholders of C corporations.

In order to make an election to be treated as an S corporation, the following requirements must be met:

- Must be an eligible entity (a domestic corporation, or a limited liability company)

- Must have only one class of stock

- Must not have more than one hundred shareholders
    - Spouses are automatically treated as a single shareholder. Families, defined as individuals descended from a common ancestor, plus spouses and former spouses of either the common ancestor or anyone lineally descended from that person, are considered a single shareholder as long as any family member elects such treatment.

- Shareholders must be U.S. citizens or residents, and must be natural persons, so corporate shareholders and partnerships are generally excluded. However, certain trusts, estates, and tax-exempt corporations, notably 501(c)(3) corporations, are permitted to be shareholders.

- Profits and losses must be allocated to shareholders proportionately to each one's interest in the business.

LLLP (Limited Liability Limited Partnership)—from Wikipedia—LLLP is a relatively new—as of this writing—modification of the limited partnership, a form of business entity recognized under U.S. commercial law. An LLLP is a limited partnership and as such consists of one or more general partners and one or more limited partners. The general partners manage the LLLP, while typically the limited partners only have a financial interest.

The difference between an LLLP and a traditional LP is with respect to the general partner's liability for the debts and obligations of the limited partnership. In a traditional limited partnership, the general partners are jointly and severally liable for the debts and obligations of the limited partnership; limited partners are not liable for those debts and obligations beyond the amount of their respective capital contributions.

In an LLLP, by having the limited partnership make an election under state law, the general partners are afforded limited liability for the debts and obligations of the limited partnership that arise during the period that the LLLP election is in place.

Which classification is right for your company?

Only you can answer that question. I recommend that you consult with a qualified tax accountant/CPA. He or she will be able to review your specific situation and offer advice on which is best from a tax-reporting standpoint.

Based on my experience, most entrepreneurs (at least initially) set their company up as either a sole proprietorship or an LLC.

If the liability (risk) is minimal for the business you are in, you may elect to set up the business as a sole proprietor and convert to an LLC when the business revenue reaches $50,000 annually or when you hire your first employee.

If the liability (risk) is significant or you have employees, you may choose to set up the business as an LLC to help manage the risk.

If you pursue a partnership, you *must* address three critical questions prior to entering into business:

1. Who is in charge?
2. Do we agree on fundamental values?
3. How will company assets be divided if the partnership is dissolved?

I don't personally recommend partnerships. All too often they end tragically over a business dispute. At a minimum you should address the questions above and enter into a formal contract outlining the understanding between the parties. Make sure both parties have the right to dissolve or discontinue the partnership in the event of a dispute. The agreement should also cover the time frame and process for distributing assets in the event one or more of the partners elects to discontinue the relationship.

Regardless of the organizational structure you will want to secure additional liability insurance coverage to help protect you from an unfortunate event. I recommend a minimum coverage threshold of $1 million per occurrence.

As we leave this topic, I want to reiterate the importance of separating your personal bank accounts from your business accounts. This will help to ensure total separation of personal and business transactions. The last thing you want is for someone to pierce the corporate veil and get to your personal assets because you are commingling your personal and business accounts.

CHAPTER 6

Office Space

Rent Versus Own

This question ranks just under capitalization: "Should I purchase a building or rent office space?"

First and foremost you have to look at your budget and cash flow. You do *not* need to purchase a building unless you have the cash to a) purchase the building outright, or b) easily manage the monthly rent out of your business budget.

There is, however, a key benefit to renting. The landlord has to pay for all repairs if you have negotiated such in your lease. Keep in mind that building owners are in this business to make money. That means all repair costs are built into the monthly rental payment.

If you own, then you are responsible for replacing carpets, repairing leaks, and repairing or replacing the roof every fifteen to twenty years. While ownership may be more attractive based on the monthly payment, you must factor in the cost of repairs and maintenance over the life of the building.

But, if you rent for a long period of time, you could be losing money. Why?

- Because you aren't building equity in the asset
- Because you aren't getting tax deductions (depreciation expense and maintenance)

TIP: MANY RENTERS ARE CONVINCED THEY ARE "BEATING THE SYSTEM" BECAUSE THEY DON'T HAVE TO PAY FOR

MAINTENANCE AND REPAIR, WHEN IN REALITY THE COSTS ARE ALL BUILT INTO THEIR RENT PAYMENT.

So, which solution is best for you?

It really depends on your cash flow and long-term goals. Renting provides far more flexibility because you can move to a larger facility or different location without first having to sell your existing building. This is a major (and legitimate) reason *not* to own.

There are other variables to consider in the small business setting. For instance, does your business depend upon exposure to specific traffic? Most retailers find it easier to rent because the cost of properties near high-traffic areas that offer visible exposure are quite costly.

For other companies such as manufacturing, which requires extensive outfitting, the benefits of ownership may outweigh renting.

In a typical rental situation, the building owner has the flexibility to keep increasing prices year after year, and most will try to lock you in to an annual lease or longer (which isn't very flexible). Likewise, you are limited on what you can do to the building without the owner's permission.

When you choose to own, you trade mobility and flexibility for a fixed asset and the associated cost of maintenance and repair.

If you enter into a rental or lease arrangement, read the fine print. Lease agreements are typically written in favor of the property owner. There are three sections to inspect:

1. Lease term
2. Termination
3. Improvements

Many lease agreements contain language allowing the agreement to automatically extend if you fail to notify the owner in writing by a specific date. Likewise, the agreement may tie you to the lease for a period of three or more years with no option for termination. If so, you are legally liable for the lease payments even if your business were to fail in the first six months.

I always recommend (when possible) negotiating a more reasonable termination provision. Examples include:

- Twelve-month lease with the option to extend for an additional twelve-month period

- Thirty-six-month lease with the option to terminate at the end of each twelve-month period without cause or penalty

- Thirty-six-month lease with the option to terminate without cause or penalty upon 120 days' written notice

The improvements section is equally important. You need to understand your rights:

- Can you paint the interior without the owner's permission?
- Can you install lighting in the facility without the owner's permission?
- Will you retain ownership of any improvements you make (lighting, fence, playground equipment, etc.)?

Virtual Office Space

Virtual offices offer a tremendous advantage to business owners who work primarily out of their home or a remote location. Virtual office space ranges from $99 per month to $150 per month for a basic package. Business owners typically get:

- Receptionist
- Toll-free phone number
- Mailbox
- Access to a fully furnished office
- Access to a fully furnished conference room

Packages vary from provider to provider, but this gives you an idea of what to expect. Depending on the package you select, you have access to office space and conference rooms for a select number of hours per month. When you need to meet with a prospective client, you schedule time in the virtual office, the office places your company nameplate on the door, and the office provides you with a polished and professional business location.

Welcome to my virtual office. How can I help you?

As I noted earlier, many entrepreneurial centers offer low-cost office space for their clients. I encourage you to evaluate your market to see if you have a center in close proximity. The resources combined with low-cost space offer a tremendous value if you do not require a formal office every day.

If you are in the professional service market, you might also consider contacting local CPAs and attorneys to see if they have a vacant office you can sublet at a reasonable cost.

As we leave this section, let me provide with you one final thought: Most entrepreneurs will opt to rent, use a virtual office, or work from home due to the cost. Until you have a solid cash flow, I would recommend against ownership. One of the biggest mistakes a business owner can make is to let his or her heart lead a purchase decision.

Entrepreneurs often work with a local real estate agent, a friend, or an acquaintance from church when they have a need for property. In many instances they spend more than they should on the transaction too.

As a general rule of thumb, find the most knowledgeable person in your market. This may be a business broker or a real estate firm. Remember, you don't have to love the person. This is just business, and you are looking for a good investment!

Analyze the options carefully and rely on the person's expertise. A good realtor will sell you a property. A great realtor will explain the pros and cons of each property you consider. Having the right realtor on your due diligence team can be the difference between a profitable portfolio and bankruptcy.

CHAPTER 7

Technology

Why do I need to use technology?

Technology is imperative for any small business in today's market. Without it you can easily fall behind on paperwork (which will be detrimental to business operations). In this section we will cover some of the most common forms of business technology. This is not intended as a definitive list but rather an overview to assist you as you map out your business plan.

Banking

At a minimum I recommend that all of your banking data be automated. I personally use Quicken to download bank transactions, although there are a host of other products on the market.

I also recommend using QuickBooks for your general ledger. For most entrepreneurs it will offer a great foundation for managing payroll, invoicing, quotes, and banking. It also allows you to produce annual profit and loss statements and other reports, which are invaluable at tax time. As your company grows, you can always consider upgrading your accounting systems. Another great option is Peachtree. You can read more about QuickBooks in the Software and Media category at http://astore.amazon.com/keystfinancon-20.

Website

I believe every business should have a web presence. That doesn't mean you have to spend a lot of money, though. Web packages come in all shapes and sizes. You can create your own website using a web design template or blog page, or you can have a professional company help you set up a site.

What do you need to get started?

- Domain name
- Web hosting service
- HTML editor

You can secure a basic site for as little as $5 month. (I can't think of a single business that isn't worth a mere $5 investment.) Domain registration will cost $10 to $12 annually. I created my first site using a web design template for less than $200, including the domain name, hosting service, and web design template.

Services can be obtained from hundreds of providers. Here is a brief list of providers offering good low-cost or free options:

- GoDaddy.com
- WordPress.com
- 1&1 Internet
- Webmasters.com
- OfficeLive.com
- Apollo Web Hosting
- Digital Peak Web Host
- Infomedia

Likewise, there are many HTML editors on the market. In fact, many of the web hosting companies will offer an editor as part of their standard management tool.

Other possible editors include:

- Dreamweaver
- Evrsoft
- FrontPage

TIP: IF YOU OPERATE A RETAIL STORE YOU CAN RE-ROUTE YOUR DOMAIN NAME TO AN ONLINE STORE USING A SITE LIKE ETSY OR EBAY AS YOUR MARKETPLACE.

There are thousands of website variations. A good business coach can often help you navigate through the maze and select a design that is right for your new business.

Find other business resources at www.RealBusinessSolutionCenter.com.

Payroll

Payroll can be handled in QuickBooks, or you can outsource the function to a professional payroll firm. If you are comfortable handling the payroll, and the process doesn't remove you from core functions within the daily operations, then by all means keep the payroll in-house.

Unfortunately for many entrepreneurs, this just isn't a reality. Outsourcing allows you to lean on the expertise of others. A simple Google search will identify those in your area; however, there are hundreds of providers in the market.

Payroll & Benefit Solutions, LLC (PBS) is a provider of outsourced payroll processing and tax filing services for small to mid-sized companies. It is headquartered in Birmingham, Alabama, but it provides payroll services in many other states. In addition to payroll processing services, it also provides human resource and benefit solutions.

ADP is another great option in the marketplace. Through its employer services product, it provides employer-related business process solutions for the smallest to largest companies. ADP provides services in the following disciplines: human resources, payroll services, mobile solutions, tax and compliance, benefits overview, workers' compensation premium payment program, pre-employment services, retirement services, Professional Employer Organization (PEO), HR business process outsourcing, procure-to-pay solutions, sales and use tax, travel and expense management, standalone services, international employer services, and medical practice services.

ADP is listed as one of the contract holders in the Member Savings Program through Real Business Solution Center. When you access its portfolio through the Member Savings Program, you save 25 percent off standard pricing. Join the free Member Savings Program at www.

RealBusinessSolutionCenter.com/small-business-purchasing-alliance/ rbsc-member-savings-program.

TIP: CPA FIRMS OFTEN PROVIDE PAYROLL SERVICES AS WELL.

Purchase Orders

QuickBooks offers a simple yet manageable process for creating quotes, purchase orders, invoices, and many other necessary business functions.

Why should you use a PO system?

Implementing a purchase order system will improve your operations immensely. Some of the more notable benefits include:

- Creates a formal process for ordering supplies
- Prevents others from placing orders without your knowledge
- Provides the vendor with a number to reference on its invoice
- Allows you to establish pay terms for accounts payable invoices
- Creates an auditable record of each transaction
- Allows you to monitor shipping terms and include additional comments
- Enables you to maintain accurate purchase, price, and stock consumption records
- Allows you to incorporate additional legal language

Shipping terms you may want to include on your purchase order include:

- Vendor pays freight
- Buyer pays freight when invoiced
- Title passes at shipping point
- Title passes at destination
- Vendor files claims (if required)
- Buyer files claims (if required)
- Vendor responsible while in transit

- Buyer responsible while in transit
- Buyer pays shipping charges when billed by carrier

Invoicing and Payment

As I noted earlier, QuickBooks offers a great low-cost option for managing your accounts payable operations. Using the purchase order system allows you to:

- Match invoices for accuracy
- Ensure the invoice price matches the quoted purchase order price
- Apply pay terms to the invoice
- Take early payment discounts

Pay terms vary from company to company; however, the most common are:

- Net 30 (30 days from the date of the invoice)
- 2% 10 (you receive a 2 percent discount if you pay the invoice within ten days of the date on the invoice)

Other pay terms you may encounter include:

- N10 (ten days from the date of the invoice)
- N20 (twenty days from the date of the invoice)
- COD (cash on delivery)
- Pay immediately (zero days from the date of the invoice)

The number of days and the discount amount can obviously vary, but this should provide you with a reasonable understanding of the general process.

By establishing pay terms, you are able to hold on to your money for a longer period of time. When you implement pay terms, you are in a position to manage your business cash flow. As with any small business, cash is king.

As a general rule, I recommend business owners set their accounts receivable terms at N15 and their accounts payable terms at N30. That means people who owe you money are required to pay within fifteen days, but you are not required to pay your suppliers for thirty days thus increasing your cash flow.

CHAPTER 8

Risk Management

Insurance

This section is not intended to be an all-inclusive discussion of insurance. I do, however, want to leave you with a few basic principles, which are outlined below:

- Workers' Compensation—Secure the statutory rate for your state.

- Renter's Insurance—If you rent your building, it is imperative that you secure renter's insurance to protect your business assets. The landlord will have insurance covering the building but, unlike your homeowner's policy, the landlord's policy will not cover your business assets. The same is true when you are renting a residence.

- Commercial General Liability Insurance—Whether you own a building, property, and equipment or you are simply in a service business, you need liability insurance to cover you in the event another person is injured on your property or by the service you provided. I generally recommend a $1 million policy with a $5 million umbrella. At a minimum you should consider personal and advertising injury, product or service liability, general aggregate (per location) and automobile liability with a minimum of $1 million per occurrence.

- Property Insurance—If you own your building, secure insurance coverage sufficient to cover the building and the internal contents from fire, theft, or other damage.

- Life Insurance—This is the category that is most often forfeited due to cash flow. That is shortsighted and can place your family at risk. If you are a sole proprietor and you lose your job due to an untimely death, then your family will no longer have the benefit of your income. I recommend that you secure a term life policy in an amount equal to eight to ten times your annual salary. This will help ensure your family is protected.

- Disability Insurance—This category is equally important. If you lose your job due to an injury or unforeseen health problem that forces you into disability, this policy will help offset the financial loss.

- Special Liability Insurance—Depending on the nature of your business, you may need a special liability policy to cover certain aspects of your business. Examples include professional liability (of the nature adequate to cover your liability arising from any design or other professional services you provide) or pollution legal liability (to be required if any specific environmental services are to be provided).

- If your company has been established as a corporation, you should also consider Executives and Officers (E&O) coverage to help protect the officers of the company from personal liability.

CHAPTER 9

Contracts

There are three basic contract categories to prepare for:

1. Contracts for products and services you provide
2. Contracts for products and services you receive
3. Competitive bids

I don't personally like contracts, but I have spent a majority of my career in contract development and supply chain management. Unfortunately, in today's society they are inevitable. There is no need for us to get into the details in this book, but I have provided several templates in the resources section of this book that you can modify and use for your new business.

When soliciting business you may also encounter competitive bids. You will hear people refer to bids in many different ways. Some of the more common terminology includes:

- RFP (Request for Proposals)—used when strict bid specifications are not required

- RFB (Request for Bid)—used when potential providers are required to meet strict specifications

- RFQ (Request for Quote)—used to secure one or more informal quotes from potential providers)

- RFI (Request for Information)—used to secure data from potential providers

Many people will use the terms interchangeably; however, each one has a distinct meaning. The key for you as a business owner is not how each entity might refer to its request, but that you complete the response appropriately. If the entity provides a strict set of specifications, you *must* respond to the request without taking exception. If you fail to do so, the entity has the right to disqualify your response from further consideration.

I generally recommend that clients respond to the initial specifications as requested and, when appropriate, provide alternate proposals that might be in the customer's best interest.

Thousands of government entities post bids every year on individual websites, as well as in local papers, corkboards, restricted feeds, and so on.

So, how do you find out where the opportunities are located?

A number of resources on the Real Business Solution Center website will help you quickly identify bid opportunities that are best suited for your business. You can quickly search the bid bulletin boards or subscribe to a national bid aggregator. Using a bid aggregator allows you to search a national bid database using preferences you establish to filter bids. Users receive a daily e-mail alert with new bids that match their user preferences. Instead of hiring an employee to search for bid opportunities or, even worse, removing yourself from other critical business functions, the bid aggregator will identify and forward bid opportunities matching your criteria. Most aggregators run around $30 monthly, far less than the cost of an employee!

Find additional information at www.RealBusinessSolutionCenter.com/opportunity-center/bid-search-engine.

CHAPTER 10

Marketing

In this section I will outline some of the more common forms of marketing, but first we need to discuss strategy!

Businesses compete in three ways: quality, service, and price. You typically get to pick *two* of the three, but not all three. Many small businesses try to play the price game. They underprice their products and services in an attempt to win business. This is a lose-lose proposition.

Small business owners simply can't compete with Walmart on price. That means you need to compete on quality and service.

Earlier we talked about your value proposition. What makes your company different from all others in the marketplace? This is where you shine, so your marketing campaign needs to highlight the benefits of using your company.

Now the challenge is finding customers. Many small businesses have a vision about who their customer is and what their customer wants, but things are seldom what they seem.

The Perfect Customer

The real challenge is identifying the "perfect customer":

- Finding them
- Keeping them
- Getting repeat sales

So how do you identify the perfect customer? The first step is to ask: "If I could choose the perfect customer, who would it be? What would my perfect customer look like?"

Many new business owners will say that anyone with money is an ideal customer. In the mind of the new business owner, all he or she wants to do is sell the product. Unfortunately, that doesn't work in most instances. If you want to focus your marketing dollars where they can do the most good, you *must* identify your ideal customer.

Your ideal customer is someone who not only wants your product or service but who can afford it and has the authority to make a purchase. Wouldn't it be great if every customer you attracted were perfect?

In this section I will provide a brief overview that will help you focus your marketing.

Who are your typical customers? What motivates them to buy?

Very few business owners take time to answer these basic questions. Yet, this is a key component to mapping out your advertising campaign and future sales initiatives.

Answering these two questions will give you a tremendous advantage in the marketplace.

Many business owners believe volume is the answer. After all, don't you want all of the business you can get? The surprising answer is no.

The key isn't in the volume of customer but the quality of customer you attract to your business. Have you ever heard of Pareto's principle, also known as the 80-20 rule?

In 1906, an Italian economist named Vilfredo Pareto created a mathematical formula to describe the unequal distribution of wealth in his country. More specifically, 20 percent of the people owned 80 percent of the wealth.

The 80-20 rule can be applied to almost anything:

- 20 percent of your employees do 80 percent of the work
- 20 percent of your inventory occupies 80 percent of your warehouse space

The same holds true for sales and marketing: 80 percent of your sales will come from 20 percent of your customers.

Your goal is to pinpoint those customers (or at least the type of customer) that represent 80 percent of your business so that you can focus your marketing efforts.

Take a moment to write down the key characteristics of your perfect customer:

_____

_____

_____

_____

_____

_____

_____

Once you have fine-tuned your definition of a perfect customer, you are ready to identify your niche and define a marketing strategy.

Finding Your Niche

When it comes to marketing, you have to find your niche, the product or service your company will provide to your perfect customer. Throughout my career as an executive with a university and as a business coach, I have encountered thousands of companies. It never ceases to amaze me how many entrepreneurs will try to be everything to everyone. They will complete vendor applications citing their proficiency in everything from lawn care to uniform sales and auto mechanics.

People will not take you seriously as a business owner until they know exactly what you can do for them and why they should choose to use your company.

Make sure you have a strong value proposition and a focused market before you open your doors. If you are an auto mechanic, your niche might be Mercedes repair services. If you are a consultant, your niche might be supply chain management.

In his book *Good to Great*, Jim Collins outlines a great principle based on Isaiah Berlin's essay "The Hedgehog and the Fox."

The essay tells a story of the wily fox who day after day plotted to catch the slow hedgehog. The hedgehog, sensing the threat, would roll up into a ball each time the fox approached, thwarting even the best offense the fox could muster.

The hedgehog in this story isn't simpleminded or stupid. It simply understands the essence of profound simplicity. It maintains focus, does its job, and wins every time.

Jim goes on to detail how this simple story applies to business, but for now I want to leave you with only one core principle: choose your niche. Do that one thing better than anyone!

If you concentrate your energy on your niche and become the best in your field, your company will succeed where so many others fail. Establish your value proposition and maintain steady focus on your perfect client base.

Steady focus will prevail

Take a few moments to define your niche in greater detail.

_____

_____

_____

_____

_____

_____

Marketing Tactics

A well-defined marketing strategy involves three elements: where, what, and how. Choosing the sales channel will tell us where we will find your perfect customer; the marketing strategy will tell us what tools we will utilize to reach them; choosing the specific tactics will tell us how.

- Where—the outreach and distribution channel you will utilize
- What—the marketing strategy you will incorporate
- How—the marketing tactic you will use (your plan)

So, which strategy is best suited for your business? Every business is different in this regard. What works for a consultant isn't necessarily appropriate for someone in retail.

First, define the primary objective of your company. More specifically, what products or services will you provide? Take a moment to write down the core focus of your new business.

_____

_____

_____

_____

_____

_____

_____

_____

Now think about your primary focus in relationship to your perfect customer. If you were the customer, what would you want? Low cost? Good quality? Great service? Will your value proposition drive your business toward your perfect customer?

Once you have identified your perfect customer and determined your value proposition to be appropriate, you are ready to focus on outreach and distribution.

So, which distribution channel is best suited for your business? There are a host of different sales channels in the market today. They include:

- Retail sales (walk-in customers)
- Phone solicitations
- Website orders
- Mail order
- Sales representatives
- Events

Next, determine which marketing strategy to incorporate. Strategies include:

- Print ads (brochures, flyers, etc.)
- Television ads
- Radio spots
- Directory ads
- Media events
- Networking events
- Billboards
- Website banners
- Speaking engagements
- Social media

Last, you have to establish a plan, the marketing tactic you will use to reach your perfect customer.

As I noted earlier, the answer varies from business to business. What works best for a retail outlet may not be appropriate for a consulting business.

It has been my experience that you need to incorporate Pareto's principle. Determine which marketing strategy will enable you to reach your perfect customer base—in other words, that 20 percent of potential customers representing 80 percent of the sales.

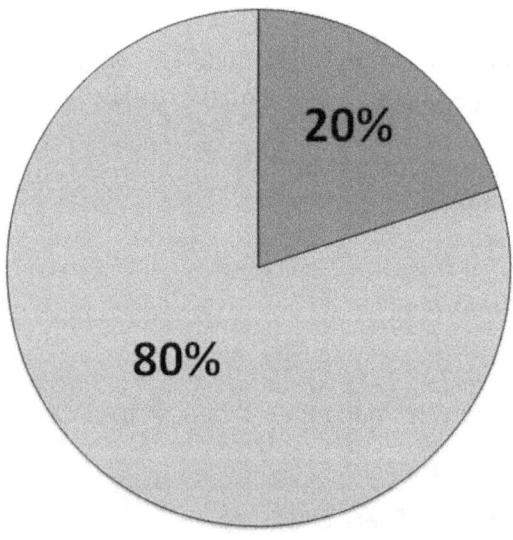

Reaching the perfect 20 percent

As a small business consultant, I have found that speaking and networking events provide the best avenue for me to reach new customers.

I feel so strongly about this that I do not subscribe to print advertising at all. I have found print advertising to be a costly form of marketing, and in most instances, it provides the least benefit.

I have heard many others over the years express the same sentiments. When they first started, they would take any speaking engagement they could find. The more they spoke, the more people they reached.

In their book *The Answer*, John Assaraf and Murray Smith draw on their many years of experience to provide an in-depth study of marketing to the perfect customer. I encourage you to pick up a copy, available at http://astore.amazon.com/keystfinancon-20, to extend your understanding in this area.

Marketing Rule of Thumb

When you engage in marketing, the idea is to reach potential clients. Right?

In order to accomplish this, you need a plan that will allow you to saturate your core market. You want to achieve what is called "top-of-mind awareness." When potential clients realize they have a need for the product or service you provide, you want your company name to be the first one that comes to their mind. You want your product or service to be on the top of the brand ladder.

Where does your company fit on the brand ladder?

We will cover this in greater detail, but for now, just recognize that you need your company to have the top spot!

> *"You cannot climb the ladder of success dressed in the costume of failure."*
> *—Zig Ziglar*

So, how do you secure that top spot?

Your marketing strategy should allow you to saturate your ideal market. Whatever you do, *don't* use the shotgun approach. When you advertise in multiple media outlets, you limit your ability to reach saturation unless you have an unlimited marketing budget.

The key is to take your marketing budget and focus 100 percent into one or two outlets. Choose those that will best allow you to reach your perfect customer.

Ad Copy

Ad copy is nothing more than the message you include in your advertising campaign.

Nothing is as disturbing as a poorly thought-out ad campaign, one that is both dull and uninspiring. How you say something is just as important as what you say.

Your ad copy should be similar to a face-to-face sales pitch. A great ad will include the offer, but more important is the language and tone of the offer.

Many entrepreneurs get so engrossed in describing the company or products that they fail to appeal to the reader.

Let your customers feel or imagine how the product will impact them. Most importantly, appeal to the reader's ego when describing those benefits. People always buy for, or are influenced by, personal desires, selfish reasons, and self-interested motives. And guess what? It's been that way for thousands of years.

People are emotional creatures, and they always will be. Your job as an entrepreneur is to express your offer in terms that trigger emotions and push them into taking action.

Many entrepreneurs fail to recognize the power of emotion. They try to let their slogan or mission statement win over the customer. Or worse yet, they try to convince the customer how good their company is.

Ask yourself what your marketing message is.

Your marketing message should *always* grab your customers' attention. It should tell them why they should trust your company or why they should choose to do business with you rather than your competitors.

Ultimately, if you aren't able to solve the customer's problem, it really doesn't matter how good your slogan or ad campaign might be.

Here are three things you should do before you start an ad campaign:

1. Identify the problems your target market is having. What are your potential customers' frustrations and pains?
2. Present your customers with your solution to their problems. Identify how your solution will improve their problems.
3. Explain what makes you different from your competitors (your value proposition).

Remember, most people just want to know what's in it for them.

Create your ad using language that will make your customer want to know more.

Top-of-Mind Awareness

When a customer has a problem, you want your company to be the first one that comes to mind. Customers who have never used your company are unsure. To them you are an unknown. They aren't sure your product will solve their problems nor why your product or service is more appropriate than those of your competitors.

But this is where your opportunity lies.

Your opportunity is to help your customers understand as many tangible and compelling reasons why they receive a greater benefit by moving forward and making a purchase from you.

There are a number of ways you can do this. One of them is giving them reasons why: Why should they buy from you? Why should they put their faith in your company? If you can help them understand and appreciate the reasons why, your customers will be strongly bonded to your business.

It's a very powerful process, and when you implement this process, you will create such a bond with your customers that they will refer many of their friends and neighbors to you.

Why?

Because you're the only company who takes the time to educate and explain to them how things work.

Have you established top-of-mind awareness?

What about social media?

I am often asked, "What can I do to market my company, my products, and myself through social media?" The answer is easy: participate!

You have to get involved and participate on Twitter, Facebook, LinkedIn, blogs, and other social media outlets. Let's face it: if you aren't in the game, you will never be successful in this area.

Whatever you do, *never* post ads directly into social media outlets unless you know it is an accepted practice. In today's environment we receive countless unsolicited e-mails and posts citing the next big opportunity. We typically refer to these as spam. People receive so many of these that they simply turn a blind eye to the notice, and in many instances it angers them to the point they would never use your company. The same is true of e-mail campaigns, which we will talk about a little later.

For now, let's take a more detailed look at some of the more prominent social media outlets.

Facebook (www.facebook.com)—This is primarily a social media for friends and family; however, it too can offer a viable avenue for marketing. Who better to help you grow your business than those who care about you? Keeping your business name in front of your friends and their friends helps to increase their awareness of you and your products. Facebook allows you to set up a business page for your company as well. You can use this landing page to post news and comments about your business, receive fans, and link to your blog. Facebook also enables you to have your business impression appear on the sidebar of your target demographic. If you want to target single males between the ages of twenty-five and fifty, Facebook has tools that can help.

Twitter (www.twitter.com)—This is one of the newest forms of media and is a good tool to help keep your company name in front of a group of interested customers. Twitter allows you to post short notices about your business. This will help keep your business name and activity in front of additional customers.

LinkedIn (www.linkedin.com)—This is a business networking site that can be extremely beneficial. The primary purpose of the site is to allow registered users to maintain a list of contact details of people they know and trust in business. LinkedIn can then be used to find jobs, people, and business opportunities. The searchable LinkedIn Groups feature allows you to establish new business relationships by joining professional groups. These groups enhance your ability to network in that your connections are on a more personal level. Professionals are more likely to connect with you online if they are connected with you or one of your contacts on a personal level. The groups also allow interaction via online business discussions with a wide and diverse business population.

Discussion Boards (Forums)—There are thousands of online discussion boards available on the Internet. While most do not allow hard sales on their sites, they do provide you with an excellent opportunity to network. If you sell sporting goods, for example, you might register for some of the higher traffic sports sites where you can interact with potential customers. This will help you to build credibility in the market.

I treat all social media sites as an extension of my business networking. When you are online posting comments, tweeting, offering answers, or simply opening a discussion, you are engaging in a form of electronic networking. You are making contact with potential clients and keeping your business name in front of potential customers. You are not only building credibility but establishing yourself as the expert in your chosen field.

Search Engine Optimization (SEO)—I have heard many say this is a must, but I tend to disagree with the strategy for start-ups. I have never once paid for optimization, and yet my website consistently pulls up in the top of most search engines. The key is simple: content, content, content. I continue to post meaningful content to my website, blog pages, and other resources. The more meaningful the content you post to the web, the more likely you will end up on top of the list. Yes, you can pay for SEO service, but your start-up dollars are far better utilized elsewhere. Search engine optimization is, however, a great tool and should be used once you have a solid and sustainable cash flow.

Here are a few simple rules or things you should be doing to win with social media:

- Blog (like crazy)
- Create profiles (everywhere you can)
- Upload photos (everywhere you can)
- Upload videos
- Create podcasts (routinely)

- Set alerts
- Comment (on multiple blogs and forums)
- Get connected (to as many as you can)
- Explore social media (set aside at least thirty minutes per week)
- Be creative (post plenty of meaningful content to your site)

Blogging should be the first priority. Setting up a blog is easier than you think. You can use an existing resource such as Blogger.com, or you can install your own blog site by using a resource such as WordPress.

Upload photographs and videos to your website. Customers want to see real people when they visit. As my friend Justin Lukasavige frequently notes, "The days of doing business with nameless, faceless companies is a thing of the past."

Create a podcast that you can make available to your customers. The more you create, the better off you will be. There are two basic forms: audio and video. If you aren't ready to invest in a camera, you can use the free audio software that's on your computer.

Commenting is *key* if you want to increase your social media exposure. Think of it as a form of cyber networking. If you were attending a traditional networking event, you would likely approach a group and wait to introduce yourself. You wouldn't walk up to a group of people and immediately start talking. That would be rude and unacceptable. You would listen first and introduce yourself at the first opportunity. Commenting on forums, blogs, and other social media outlets should follow the same protocol. Read the blogs first and add comments when the opportunity arises.

Exploring social media is equally important. Spend at least thirty minutes a week reviewing various sites to see where you can provide comment. The more you participate in networking events (virtually or in person) and create meaningful data, the quicker you distinguish *yourself* as the expert in the market.

Remember, if you aren't in the game, you can never win!

Start-up Advertising on a Limited Budget

Start-up advertising is a major concern for most entrepreneurs, but which marketing strategy is best?

As we discussed, a well-defined marketing strategy involves three elements: where, what, and how. Where will we find our perfect customer, what tools can help us reach them, and what strategy will we choose (how)?

When you engage in marketing, the idea is to reach potential clients. Right? In order to accomplish this, you need a plan that will allow you to saturate your core market and achieve top-of-mind awareness.

So, how do you secure that top spot if you have a limited budget?

It has been stated that the half-life of advertising traffic is zero. This means that the moment you stop shelling out cash, the traffic stops. With typical conversion rates of 1 to 2 percent, you end up paying a lot of money to reach only one or two customers out of every one hundred.

Few start-ups can withstand the financial impact required to create a positive ROI (return on investment) from their advertising campaign.

So how do we combat this issue? Here are a few insights that may help!

E-mail Campaign

Offer incentives in exchange for a visitor's e-mail address (a free trial, reports, books, etc.). This will enable you to stay in contact with your customer base and will increase your conversion rate.

You can easily use resources such as Constant Contact or MailChimp to stay in contact with your e-mail subscribers.

TIP: NEVER ADD SOMEONE TO YOUR E-MAIL DISTRIBUTION LIST WITHOUT HIS OR HER PERMISSION. WE HAVE ALL BEEN BOMBARDED WITH SPAM TO THE POINT THAT MOST PEOPLE ARE OFFENDED BY THE ACTION. THE LAST THING YOU WANT TO DO AS A BUSINESS OWNER IS TO OFFEND A POTENTIAL CUSTOMER!

Pay-Per-Click Advertising

Pay-per-click advertising is simply a process where you pay a fee each time someone clicks your add.

After a short period (typically thirty to sixty days), potential customers will become desensitized. Your ad will become a normal display on the page and you will no longer command their attention.

When this happens (and it will), all of the time you invested in your ad campaign is gone!

So does this mean you shouldn't invest in pay-per-click advertising? No.

You should, however, use pay-per-click advertising to augment your primary campaign. Pay-per-click advertising is a great way to quickly increase traffic over a short period of time. Just be sure you can discontinue the campaign after a short period without penalties.

Pay-per-click advertising can also provide insight into how select traffic converts for you. As an example: Facebook has the ability to track demographics. With its reports you can quickly see that women between the ages of thirty and fifty convert at a rate of 25 percent whereas men between the ages of twenty and thirty convert at a rate of 45 percent. This is valuable information because it will help you target your perfect customer.

Remember, it isn't about reaching the most people! It is about reaching perfect customers that you can "convert" into sales!

Niche Advertising

Depending on your business niche, you can likely find a forum, blog, or website that caters to your niche. This is where you want to invest some of your advertising budget.

Niche sites will drive more target-specific traffic to your site. Get online and interact with your potential customers, answer questions, provide advice, and become their go-to advisor.

Google AdWords

People traditionally think of Google AdWords as the ads that appear to the right of the search results.

When Google AdWords was first launched, it was a tremendous resource for the business community. Markets were untouched and low-cost click rates were the norm.

Today, however, click rates are much higher and with the market saturated, the conversion rate is much lower.

If you are using Google AdWords as a marketing strategy, you should consider its content network (i.e., the ads that appear in the AdSense window). The content network is less targeted, offers higher volume, and typically offers lower cost. AdWords's Conversion Optimizer may be a good tool to consider.

Facebook Ads

Facebook still offers a viable solution for business owners. The value of Facebook is its ability to direct ads to your perfect customer.

The key to achieving a low click fee is to increase your click-through rate. In order to accomplish this, you need a powerful image, an engaging headline, and a focused target audience.

When you set up your first Facebook ad campaign, begin with a fixed daily cost you can manage. At the end of the first day, review your Facebook reports to see which ad has the highest click-through rate. Discontinue ads with a low click-through rate and increase the number of ads with the highest click-through rate.

As I noted earlier, pay-per-click advertising should never be a long-term strategy. Your niche market will tune out your ad after thirty to sixty days. When this occurs your click-through rate will drop and the per-click fee will increase.

Phone Solicitation

The phone isn't dead, but we have all grown tired of telemarketing calls. If you use phone solicitation as a marketing tool, be sure you have a clear and focused target group. Keep the call short and lead with an incentive to the customer.

Word of Mouth

The most important and effective part of any advertising campaign comes from word of mouth—customers referring your company to their friends and family.

Be sure to ask every customer to mention your business!

Print Ads (brochures, flyers, etc.)

With the exception of retail, print advertising offers a very low return on investment (ROI). Some people have even gone so far as to say that print is dead!

I receive countless flyers and marketing materials in the mail, and I have become so desensitized to them that I *never* look at a single advertisement. I immediately toss them in the trash. If you invest any of your limited marketing dollars on print advertising, make sure it is targeted to your perfect customer.

Television Ads and Radio Spots

There is a definite venue for TV and radio advertising; however, the cost is often prohibitive for most start-up companies. A typical TV campaign can start at $30,000 annually and only goes up from there. If your budget is sufficient to cover the cost, a well-defined campaign can help you quickly saturate your local market.

Directory Ads

Directory ads offer little value. In today's market when you need a resource, do you pull out a paper phone directory, or do you look up the resource on the computer?

If you look up the resource on the computer, do you use one of the standard directory resources, or do you perform a Google search?

Most business owners today will say they use a Google search. If that is the case, why would you ever want to spend any of your precious marketing dollars in paper or electronic directory listings?

If you are searching for resources online, then odds are most others are as well.

TIP: RURAL AREAS ARE THE EXCEPTION BECAUSE INTERNET MAY NOT BE AS READILY AVAILABLE.

I should also note that directory ad contracts are often burdensome for the small business owner. Some firms embed language in their standard agreement requiring the business owners to send a cancellation notice, written in a specific manner, to a specific location, by a predefined date. If the business owner misses the date by even one day, or fails to comply with the instructions exactly, the contract is automatically renewed for another year. Before you enter into *any* arrangement, I recommend that you first conduct a Google search on the firm to see if there are complaints or, even worse, evidence of a scam.

Networking Events

Networking events offer little value from a conversion standpoint. They do, however, provide you with access to quality contacts. My recommendation for any networking event is merely to socialize, ask questions, and collect business cards. Once the event is over, make contact with everyone you met and schedule a follow-up meeting. This will enable you to have a well-defined business conversation and determine how you can best work with the contact.

TIP: THIS IS *NOT* AN OPPORTUNITY TO SELL THEM ON YOU OR YOUR COMPANY.

Remember, ultimately business is still relational. Establish (and maintain) a relationship with your perfect customer.

Here are some suggestions on being proactive at a networking event. I have found that if you ask the questions you want someone to ask you, you will build trust. So if you want someone to ask you a specific question, ask it first.

Here are a few questions you can massage to fit your business:

- What is your target market?
- What is your biggest challenge?
- How do you generate most of your business?
- What sets you apart from your competition?
- What type of customer would be a great prospect for you?

The last question is the best because it lets them know you are interested in referring business to them. By doing this, they are likely to ask you the same question. The next time you are at a networking event, use these questions and see what happens.

BNI International

BNI is a membership-based networking organization and is one of the largest business networking organizations in the world. It offers members the opportunity to share ideas, contacts, and business referrals. The philosophy of this organization is built upon the idea that by giving business to others, you will get business in return. Its mission is to help members increase their business through a structured, positive, and professional word-of-mouth program.

Billboards

Billboards can be effective but, like pay-per-click advertising, should be used for short periods of time. After thirty to sixty days, viewers will become desensitized and simply ignore or tune out your message. To have a truly effective billboard campaign, rotate your message to multiple billboards at least once every ninety days. Billboard campaigns are typically higher in cost and may or may not reach your target audience.

Direct Mail

With direct mail the challenge is tracking results. Your cost is fixed and typically offers a low conversion rate. Direct mail *can* be effective if you can easily target your perfect customer.

Text Marketing

This is one of the latest trends. Using a resource such as iZigg, you can send text messages directly to the people who will buy your products and services.

Other resources you may want to check out include:

- Craigslist
- StumbleUpon
- Reddit
- ClickTale
- Crazy Egg
- InfluAds
- BuySellAds

- Gamezebo
- VentureLoop
- TechCrunch
- Vator
- Cheezburger Network
- iShirtUp
- vADz

Marketing Strategy Made Easy

Remember our mantra: failing to plan means planning to fail.

Every major event in life needs a solid plan. Would you expect your contractor to begin construction on your new home without a blueprint? Of course not!

Marketing is no different. Your overall marketing plan should cover a period of six to twelve months and should include weekly or monthly milestones.

Here are a few simple tips:

1. Establish a marketing budget. How much money can you reasonably afford to spend on marketing?

We all know marketing costs money. The amount of money you are willing to commit will help determine which strategy is best. Remember, you want to be economical, but you also need to be realistic on what it will take to reach your perfect customer.

2. Identify your target market.

Who is your perfect customer (the customer who is most likely to buy your product or service)? This is the customer you want to reach. As we learned earlier, a common mistake business owners make is assuming everyone is in their target group. Unfortunately, there is no product that appeals to every person.

3. Select the media outlet you will use to reach your perfect customer (social media, direct mail, television, radio, e-mail lists, etc.).

Your decision will depend largely on your budget and target audience. Choose one or two media outlets that will allow you to saturate your target market and secure top-of-mind awareness.

If you use an e-mail list, the first rule is *never* to send spam. Only send ads to those who have specifically given their permission or opted in to your list. Otherwise, you run the risk of alienating potential customers.

There are hundreds of lists available in the market. I don't recommend purchasing an existing list, because those included have not opted in to receive your advertisement. If, however, you decide to purchase an existing list, there are a number of considerations:

- Talk to other people who have purchased mailing lists from the company.
- Is there a guarantee on delivery of valid e-mail addresses? You want to make sure the list contains a relatively high percentage of valid addresses.
- Having a guarantee will help ensure the company routinely updates or validates data.

4. Establish a marketing schedule and stick with it. For example:

- How many times per month will you send out a direct mail advertisement?
- How long will you run a billboard ad?
- How long will you run a pay-per-click ad campaign?
- How many times per week and how long will you post to discussion forums?

The importance of your marketing strategy cannot be stressed enough. As with your business plan, develop a marketing strategy and revisit it often!

CHAPTER 11

Selling

Selling is a process, so don't be surprised when people fail to return your phone call or you run into a brick wall. Success typically comes when you make contact with individuals. If you are leaving messages and they aren't returning your calls, you have to ask yourself why.

Is it your message, your tone, or your timing? *Always* leave a message that makes them want to call you back.

If a potential customer fails to respond, you have to thank him or her for the opportunity and move on to the next call. Every *no* brings you that much closer to a *yes*!

We will talk about selling techniques in greater detail, but for now let's focus on the three primary components of a sale: probing, objection handling, and closing.

When you begin to probe, you are attempting to identify client needs. In order to get customers to relay the information, you have to ask more questions, such as, "How can I help you? What specifically are you looking for?" Use statements that let them know you aren't trying to be pushy; you just really want to provide a product or service that meets their needs.

TIP: ONE THING THAT MAY HELP IS TO BE FAMILIAR WITH THE PERSONALITY PROFILE WE DISCUSSED EARLIER. IF YOU IDENTIFY THE PROSPECTIVE CUSTOMER'S PERSONALITY TYPE AND COMMUNICATE ACCORDINGLY, YOUR SUCCESS RATE WILL LIKELY IMPROVE.

Objection handling is merely the art of overcoming objections. The idea is to break down any barriers your potential customers have set up. If it is pricing, then let them know the price is negotiable, providing there is room in your margin. If their hesitation is related to your competition, let them know how you differ. Focus on your value proposition.

Closing is the final phase. This is where you hope to be rewarded with an order.

Many of the sales techniques used today date back to the 1920s. Does that surprise you? Very little has changed in the sales process. Let's take a moment to break down a typical sales call.

Many salespeople will open a sales call by appealing to clients on a personal level. They talk about their personal interests, family, or favorite sport and slowly begin to ask probing questions about their business using open-ended questions.

An open-ended question is one that can't be answered with a simple yes or no. It requires the customer to provide a lengthier response. Examples of open-ended questions are: Why is that important to you? What are your goals? What are you trying to accomplish?

Next, they lay out the benefits of their product or service. Let customers know how it will impact them personally and how it will solve a problem they have to deal with.

Then deal with any objections the customer raises and close the deal.

Simple, right?

The reality is that sales is one of the most critical components in business. Large corporations spend thousands of dollars sending their representatives for sales training. They recognize the importance of selling!

So, how can you turn your employees into an award-winning sales team?

The first step is to help them understand their role in the process. A great salesperson understands his or her role is that of a problem solver. If you can solve a customer's problems, then there is very little selling involved.

In his book *SPIN Selling*, Neil Rackham discusses this issue in great detail. He states the sales process has four primary stages: preliminaries, investigating, demonstrating ability, and obtaining commitment.

He identifies four types of questions that should be used during the various stages of the sales process:

- Situation questions
- Problem questions
- Implication questions
- Need-payoff questions

Situation questions are based on facts related to the buyer's existing situation (e.g., "How long have you had your equipment?").

Problem questions focus on how an issue affects the buyer on a personal level while clarifying the problem (e.g., "Are you concerned about the quality your current equipment provides?").

Implication questions typically outline the impact of the problem while noting the seriousness of the situation. The intent is to increase the buyer's motivation to change (e.g., "What effect will the quality have on your customer satisfaction?").

Need-payoff questions are intended to get the buyer to relay his or her needs and acknowledge how your product will positively impact the situation. Getting the buyer to restate the benefits of your product will have a much greater impact, and you don't come off as a pushy salesman.

An excerpt from *SPIN Selling* says it well: "…effective planning takes you more than halfway to effective execution."

You can purchase a copy of Neil Rackham's book at http://astore.amazon.com/keystfinancon-20.

Remember, these are techniques as opposed to a rigid formula. Treat it as a simple selling guide. Treating it as a rigid step-by-step guide is a sure formula for failure.

To be an effective salesperson, you *must* first recognize your role. Then implement some of the strategies outlined above.

Simple Selling Tips

- Practice one sales technique at a time.

- Use each technique multiple times so you will become comfortable with the process.

- Never send generic e-mails.

- If you are reaching out by phone, leave a message and then call again at a later time. If you still don't receive a response, then send a short e-mail letting the client know you are available.

- Mail a formal letter outlining your service, especially your value proposition. End the letter by telling the client you will call his or her office on a specific date to schedule a meeting. Once the client has had time to receive the letter, place a call and try to coordinate a formal meeting.

- Remember, business is still relational. The stronger your relationship with your client, the greater success you will have.

- Don't get discouraged if the client isn't interested. I have had clients call me six months later. They were ready for my help!

- If you call and receive a message that the client's mailbox is full and you can't leave a message, immediately send a personalized e-mail mentioning any specific needs he or she may have mentioned. End the e-mail with, "Call me at your earliest convenience. We have a solution that I think you will be interested in."

Sales Database

This is something that few small business owners use. Create a database to capture relevant information on your customers. When a new customer contacts you via your website, ask them what search terms they used to find you or which search terms they used that didn't work. You can take this information and use it to refine the keywords on your website.

Using that same logic, each time a customer makes a purchase, enter the transaction in the database and then have an employee call to thank him or her for being your customer. Your employee can also ask why the customer purchased from you and not the competition. This information will prove invaluable when you are creating your next ad campaign.

Professional Service Model

What if you aren't in the retail business? You have no products to sell, so how can "selling" work for your business?

Service providers utilize selling techniques more than you might think. You need to:

- Identify client needs
- Demonstrate how your services will benefit the client
- Most important, close the sale

Service providers who implement a solid sales strategy can easily earn $100,000 or more. Is it easy? Of course, the answer is no—not without putting in a lot of work.

If, however, you are willing to put in the effort, you can achieve success using the selling technique outlined above.

In his book *Become a Coach*, Justin Lukasavige provides a "6 Figure Coaching Model" that can be modified to meet most any service business. Justin outlines the following:

- Work with ten new clients (average of $650) per month = $78,000
- Sell five DISC profiles each month ($30 each) = $1,800
- Conduct six group coaching sessions per year with six people each ($450) = $16,200
- Conduct ten workshops per year with twenty people each at $27 = $5,400
- Offer a high-value info product on your website at $10. Sell ten per month = $1,200
- Total: Over $100,000 per year

Looks easy, right?

The numbers are laid out and they make sense, but as I'm sure you have already realized, it's not an easy process. The key is to build in multiple revenue streams and put in a lot of work!

Finding and engaging potential clients is the key. So, where and how do you find clients?

As a professional service provider, the four most powerful things you can do are:

1. Have a website.
2. Write as much as you can (blogs, articles, etc.).
3. Speak wherever someone will let you.
4. Use the marketing tools in this book.

The key is to only work with a limited number of clients each month. Using Pareto's principle you only work with your perfect customer (the 20 percent of your clients that will produce 80 percent of your revenue).

Instead of charging a small fee to a lot of people, you charge a higher fee and work with select clients.

When you are no longer working to convert every person you come in contact with, you can put more time into those who are the best fit. Your clients will love this and will gladly pay more to be a part of it.

Your time is valuable, so you don't need to waste time with people who aren't willing to do what it takes. If your motivation is to truly serve people, you should be able to enjoy what you do and be compensated well for your work.

The key is to take action!

You might ask, "What if I get nervous in front of big groups?"

Speaking engagements and group workshops are the two best ways to get started and to build a reputation in the community. Don't let big groups stand in the way of becoming successful. Create a short PowerPoint presentation (twenty to thirty minutes in length) and try to get on the calendar with some of the local civic groups, such as Chambers or Rotary Clubs.

The more you get in front of people, the quicker you become the area expert!

Speaking Tips

I recognize there is an element of teaching involved, but it is important to invite participants to engage in the conversation. This will help build a network of like minds. The audience will come together and build off each other. You will begin to create excitement and enthusiasm. It's contagious.

I have walked in to presentations thinking I would get thirty minutes only to be told I had eight minutes, or given fifteen minutes and then later told one-and-a-half hours. Here are a few suggestions to help you stay flexible:

- Find out as much as you can about your audience, so you can speak to their concerns. This is how you should craft your talk.

- Gather your energy before each presentation.

- Stay low-tech. Creating a detailed PowerPoint presentation takes time, and you might find your laptop and projector not working the day you present. Instead, hand out a one-page outline with space for people to take notes. Don't put too much information on the outline or your audience may read instead of listening to you.

- Engage with your audience. Talk with them, not to them. Allow the audience to engage with each other. Always use a mixed format: talking is for auditory learners, and the one-page outline works for visual and kinesthetic learners.

- Start your presentation with a question or series of questions that allow for the audience to raise their hands. This is a great way to immediately engage your audience.

- Use stories and jokes in lieu of excess data. People remember much more when the content is embedded in a story. Charts are good but tend to get boring rather quickly.

- Close your presentation with a call to action.

- Try to keep the audience focused on the value of setting goals as opposed to rehashing problems.

- Never leave a meeting without next steps or assignments.

TIP: DON'T EXPECT PEOPLE TO AUTOMATICALLY BECOME CLIENTS JUST BECAUSE YOU GIVE A PRESENTATION. PEOPLE ARE BUSY. THIS IS WHY YOUR ONE-PAGE SHEET NEEDS TO HAVE YOUR CONTACT INFO OR AT LEAST E-MAIL ADDRESS ON IT. I ALSO ENCOURAGE YOU TO SOLICIT EACH AUDIENCE MEMBER'S E-MAIL ADDRESS FOR YOUR NEWSLETTER. THIS WILL ALLOW YOU TO STAY IN FRONT OF THE CUSTOMER AS TIME PASSES.

As we close this section I want to leave you with three simple rules:

1. Diversify—Incorporate multiple revenue streams into your financial business model.

2. Pareto's principle—Work with your perfect customers.

3. Fire imperfect customers who are more of a drain on your resources than the benefit they provide.

TIP – YOU CAN USE CLICKBANK TO GAIN ACCESS TO OTHER RESOURCES YOU CAN SELL ON YOUR SITE TO CREATE ADDITIONAL REVENUE STREAMS.

> *"The only place success comes before work is in the dictionary."*
> *—Vince Lombardi*

CHAPTER 12

Managing Your Bottom Line

By now you should have a good understanding of revenue streams and how important they are to your bottom line. Just as with personal finance, income is your number one wealth-building tool.

To manage or strengthen your bottom line, you need to bring in as much revenue as possible. But is that where you stop?

Absolutely not!

As you have already learned, you need to:

- Create a realistic budget and manage the income you have.

- Set aside three to six months' worth of business expenses in an emergency savings or money market account.

- Revisit your operations and eliminate unnecessary tasks.

- Review how you spend your time and outsource functions better served by someone else.

- Employ sales techniques to increase revenue.

- Implement a structured marketing strategy to reach your perfect customer.

What we haven't discussed are group purchasing organizations (GPOs) or consortia contracts. While most GPOs serve a specific market such as health care, there are a few available to the small business community.

GPOs typically use the combined purchasing volume from their membership to negotiate or leverage greater discounts for members. By joining a GPO, business owners gain significant purchasing power. They are able to secure discounts well below anything they would be able to negotiate on their own.

One of the best organizations Real Business Solution Center has identified is The Buying Group. In fact, we felt so strongly about the organization that we included them as a resource in our Member Savings Program.

By registering as a member of the Member Savings Program, you are able to access a collaborative purchasing alliance representing more than 250,000 businesses. Leading vendors are attracted to the group and make significant discounts available because of the overall business the group brings them.

You can register to participate by visiting www.RealBusinessSolutionCenter.com/small-business-purchasing-alliance/rbsc-member-savings-program.

The best part of all—it's free! We have negotiated an arrangement that will enable our members to assess the portfolio at no cost.

As of the writing of this book, the Member Savings Program portfolio includes but is not limited to:

- Air Ambulance—emergency transportation
- Armstrong Relocation—moving and storage
- Asset Management Solutions—asset management software and services
- Career Cruising—résumé builder, career assessments, and job search
- Stewart Organization—Canon copy and fax machines
- Office Depot—office supplies
- RBS WORLDPAY—credit card processing
- PODS: Portable On Demand Storage—moving and storage
- Transworld Systems/Experian—collection agency and credit reporting
- Global Solutions Inc.—telecom auditing
- J. Smith Lanier—insurance for businesses

- Grainger—industrial/facility safety, tools, and supplies
- HR Screening Inc.—tax credits for new hires
- ADP—payroll processing
- Pre Paid Legal Inc.—legal services
- Lifelock—identity theft protection
- Capitol Marketing Concepts—rewards programs for employees and customers
- WebEx—tele/Web conferences
- Constant Contact—e-mail marketing
- New Benefits—free discount pharmacy card
- Assurant Health—non-employer-sponsored health insurance plans
- Epic Hearing Savings Plan—hearing savings plan
- Liberty Mutual—home and auto insurance
- Thrifty Rental Car— Auto Rental
- CeXchange—recycling of consumer electronics

I encourage you to join and start saving today!

CHAPTER 13

Management

Management means a lot of different things to a lot of different people. Some believe managing is to stand over an employee; others believe you should empower the people. In fact, management involves supervising employees, managing operations, and even managing your personal time.

Wikipedia defines management as follows: "Management in all business and human organization activity is the act of getting people together to accomplish desired goals and objectives. Management comprises planning, organizing, staffing, leading or directing, and controlling an organization (a group of one or more people or entities) or effort for the purpose of accomplishing a goal. Resourcing encompasses the deployment and manipulation of human resources, financial resources, technological resources, and natural resources."

In other words, management is whatever it takes to get the job done!

There are many different methods of managing operations and staff.

In their book *The One Minute Manager*, Kenneth Blanchard and Spencer Johnson present a management road map that is built on a simple yet compelling model:

*   Set goals
*   Praise staff
*   Reprimand staff

The model they have outlined offers one of the best models I have found. I have implemented similar practices throughout my personal career, and they *work*!

60 seconds to better management

It is critical for you to establish expected goals. If an employee doesn't know what is expected of him or her, the employee's performance may not meet your expectations. Sit down with your employees (or outsourced professionals) and make sure they understand your requirements. Write everything down and place it in a policy manual so everyone will have access to the same information.

If your employees exceed your expectations, be quick to praise them for their accomplishments.

Likewise, if they fail to meet your expectations, you should reprimand them.

A key component of the reprimand is presentation. Don't belabor the issue. Simply make the employee aware of his or her failure, make sure the employee knows where the policy manual is kept, and then praise the employee as a person.

That's right—praise them as a person.

> *"A soft word turns away wrath." (Proverbs 15:1)*

Let him or her know that you value them as a person and as an employee, that you are not upset with him or her as a person but rather his or her failure to meet the expected level of performance.

I am not an advocate of lording over employees. I believe it creates a negative mind-set and ultimately leads to poor performance. Don't get me wrong; some employees need oversight, some might even prefer it, but your management style can't be one-sided.

Remember these four guiding principles:

- Provide clear expectations
- Encourage good performance
- Reprimand bad performance
- Provide career counseling

You might ask, "Why would I provide career counseling? Didn't they hire on to do a specific job?"

The short answer is this: Sometimes people will accept a job or even a promotion based solely on the salary. Once they begin to do the work, they find that they are unqualified or, even worse, they are miserable. When this occurs you will often see it in their work. It isn't that they are bad employees; they are simply in the wrong job.

- Perhaps they need to be in another position.

- Perhaps they need additional training.
- Perhaps they just need to get off the bus.

A business is like a bus headed toward a specific destination. If that isn't where you want to go, you may want to consider getting off the bus at the next stop.

Is it time for you to get off the bus?

By providing career counseling, you can help those individuals find out where they need to be placed.

You are in a position as a manager to help them with career decisions that will lead them to a passionate career.

Helping someone off the bus isn't a bad thing if it is handled the right way!

I had to wake up an employee so I could fire him several years ago. No, I don't mean the employee was merely dozing at his desk. This employee had gone into a vacant office, turned off the lights, closed the door, curled up on the floor behind the desk, and gone to sleep. Add an alarm clock and a pillow and he was set for the night!

The reality is that this employee was not a bad person he was merely dissatisfied with where he was in his career and with what he was doing. He had no passion for the job. It was time to get off the bus and into a career he would be happy with.

Have your employees take a personality profile test to establish their strengths and weaknesses. Use the career questions in the front of this book to identify their passions, and then make the free Career Cruising resource available. Notice I said your *employees* as opposed to a single employee.

Let all of your employees know you want them to be successful. You will be amazed at the reaction!

By making the Career Cruising resource available, you are providing them with a tremendous company benefit that will cost you absolutely nothing but a little time.

If you find termination is the only viable solution I recommend a three phased approach.

Phase I – Verbal Warning (Identify the issue)

Phase II – Formal Written Warning (citing failure to adhere to policy)

Phase III – Dismissal for cause

TIP – BEFORE YOU IMPLEMENT A FORMAL DISMISSAL PROCESS IT IS ESSENTIAL THAT YOU FIRST CREATE AND POST A FORMAL POLICY ON EMPLOYEE CONDUCT INCLUDING PENALTIES FOR ABUSE.

> *"You don't lead by hitting people over the head—that's assault, not leadership."*
> *—Dwight D. Eisenhower*

You can purchasea copy of *The One Minute Manager* at http://astore.amazon.com/keystfinancon-20.

Time Management

This is a critical component within any business. As the owner you simply can't be involved in every aspect of the operation. Likewise, you can't spend all of your time writing blogs and posting information on social media outlets.

Write down all of the activities you are involved in and then scrutinize your activity. You want to focus 80 percent of your time on those tasks that 1) you are best suited to handle and 2) that will positively impact your business.

Earl Bakken, founder of Medtronic (one of the world's largest manufacturers of pacemakers and implantable devices), had a saying: "Ready, fire, aim!"

The key is to avoid getting bogged down in the process. When you have a product or service line ready to launch, fire first and then take aim (correcting minor issues) after you go live. If you waste too much of your time trying to get the product or service perfect, you may miss critical opportunities.

In simpler terms:

- Ready—when you see a need
- Fire—get started
- Aim—adjust your aim (refine your product or service)

As I noted earlier, you must also employ the power of positive quitting. As a manager you need to recognize when it is time to quit. This may be as simple as having employees discontinue an unproductive task or closing the business entirely.

It takes most new businesses eighteen to twenty-four months to ramp up (from concept to inception).

If your company does not have sufficient cash flow to cover expenses at the end of twenty-four months, you need to seriously evaluate closing as one of your options.

The Law of Success

The Law of Success in 16 Lessons, published in 1925, is the title of Napoleon Hill's first book. The project was commissioned by Andrew Carnegie and is based on interviews of more than five hundred American millionaires over two decades, including self-made industrial giants Henry Ford, J. P. Morgan, John D. Rockefeller, Alexander Graham Bell, and Thomas Edison.

The laws are simple, but they convey a business and management style that is as relevant today as it was in 1925:

1. A business *master mind* is developed through the cooperation of two or more people who ally themselves for the purpose of accomplishing a given task.
2. A *definite chief aim* urges people to discover their natural talents, then organize, coordinate, and put into use the knowledge gained from experience. One of the primary reasons people fail is they have no definitive aim in life. They fail to set clear and attainable goals or establish plans to accomplish these goals.
3. *Self-confidence* is the realization that you can do it if you believe you can.
4. The *habit of saving* deals with money. Saving is merely a matter of habit. It is critical that you start and maintain a good habit of managing your business and personal finances.
5. *Initiative and leadership* deal with qualities necessary for the attainment of success. Leaders exercise initiative, have a definite purpose in mind, and possess self-confidence.
6. *Imagination*. Don't be afraid to dream big dreams. Let your imagination and creative spirit guide your vision.
7. *Enthusiasm*. Let your passion for the business shine through. Enthusiasm is one of the most important factors in sales and management. The best part is, it's contagious.
8. *Self-control*. Hill states that without self-control, your enthusiasm "resembles the unharnessed lightning of an electrical storm—it may strike anywhere; it may destroy life and property. Enthusiasm arouses action, and self-control directs that action in a constructive way." Self-control will enable you to control your actions and the tendency to spend more than you earn.

9. *The habit of doing more than paid for.* I think this one speaks for itself. Always give the customer more than they expect. This one act will help ensure you get repeat business and, best of all, referrals!

10. *A pleasing personality.* You must have a personality that attracts, one in which you take a genuine interest in other people and form a relationship. Think about your perfect customer or your employee. What can you do to form a stronger relationship?

11. *Accurate thinking* involves two things: separating fact from erroneous information and separating fact into two classes, relevant and irrelevant.

12. *Concentration of attention* means focusing the mind on a given desire until ways and means for its realization have been worked out.

13. *Cooperation* is the beginning of any organized effort. Hill discusses two forms of cooperation. The first is cooperation between people who group themselves together or form alliances for the purpose of attaining a given end (the master mind group). The second form of cooperation is between the conscious and the subconscious minds of an individual, or what he calls infinite intelligence. He mentions that nearly all successful businesses are conducted under some form of cooperation, and cooperation is the foundation of all successful leadership. The point Hill emphasizes is this: It is vital for individuals to surround themselves with people who have the talents and skills that they themselves lack. No one succeeds alone.

14. *Profiting by failure.* Hill gives a different slant on the word failure. He states that failure is normally a negative word, but he distinguishes failure from temporary defeat, and temporary defeat can be a blessing in disguise. There ultimately is no failure. What appears to be failure is usually a minor setback in disguise.

15. *Tolerance.* Intolerance clouds the mind and stops moral, mental, and spiritual development. Simply put, regardless of your business, cooperation and tolerance can be of tremendous help in achieving one's definite chief aim.

16. The *Golden Rule* essentially means do unto others as you would have them do unto you if your positions were reversed. Hill stresses the fact that all of your actions and thoughts will come back to you, for better or worse. Hill tells us that it is not enough to merely believe in the philosophy of the Golden Rule; one must apply it.

CHAPTER 14

Employees

Should you hire employees?

The answer is very business specific and often presents the greatest challenge to new business owners.

There are several options you can consider:

- Operate as a sole proprietor—You are the only employee in this instance.
- Contract for specific services—You outsource specific functions to other independent contractors or businesses.
- Hire employees—You hire employees to run the daily operations and pay them through a traditional payroll.

There are of course advantages and disadvantages to each. If you are a sole proprietor, you end up doing everything yourself. While this may be fine in the beginning, there will come a time when you simply don't have enough hours in the day. At some point (and only you can decide when), you will need to either outsource specific functions or hire employees. If you outsource the function, you pay another individual (or company) to do the work for you. In this instance you will not be managing their work. They will determine how to best accomplish the task you have contracted with them. You will simply pay them a fee for a specific result.

If you hire employees, you will be required to perform additional tasks. This could include running payroll, deducting and reporting tax, workers' compensation, benefits (vacation, retirement, health care, etc.) supervising, and quality control.

As we discussed earlier, you as the owner should focus your time and energy on those aspects of the business that you are best suited to handle. The other components need to be outsourced, or you need to hire employees with the expertise.

There is no cookie-cutter method that will satisfy every need. You must define the scope of your operation and whether you can or should operate without employees. As a consultant you may not need formal employees, but if you own a retail operation or a food franchise, it will be imperative.

Consult with your CPA to see which option is best for your specific situation.

CHAPTER 15

Exit Strategy

Nobody likes to think about exiting when you are just getting started, but having an exit plan is a must for any new business.

I have had entrepreneurs ask me why they need to create an exit strategy. They felt as if they were admitting defeat before they got started.

That couldn't be further from the truth. Having an exit strategy doesn't mean your business will fail. Even the most successful businesses need to have an exit strategy.

Yes, it is possible that your business will fail, and you need to plan for that, but the real reason to have a comprehensive exit strategy is to preserve the business. I will cover both in greater detail.

Failed Business

Your exit strategy should include a section outlining your strategy for closing the business in the event the venture is unsuccessful. I generally recommend an initial three-to-six-month window. As an example your plan might call for closing or re-evaluating business operations if you fail to make a sale by the end of the sixth month.

The IRS considers your business to be a hobby if you fail to turn a profit at the end of the third year. As such, you are no longer allowed to claim a loss after the third year.

Only you can decide what tolerance level is right for you. At a minimum, your exit strategy should include milestones. I have found the following time periods provide a solid base: three months, six months, nine months, twelve months, twenty-four months, and thirty-six months.

At least one of the milestones should call for the business to close. Examples might include:

- Close the business if we have not made a sale by the end of the twelfth month.

- Close the business if we have not turned a profit by the end of the third year.

Successful Business

You should also include a section outlining your strategy for a successful business. More specifically, what will happen to the business if:

- You decide to retire?
- You become mentally or physically incapacitated?
- You die prematurely?

Some of the more widely used strategies include:

- Close the business; sell the assets and shut the doors.

- Sell the business to a new owner who will continue to run the business like you did.

- Allow the business to be acquired by another company in the same or similar industry.

- Pass on the business to a spouse or children for them or a hired manager to run.

Regardless of the strategy you ultimately choose, the important thing is that you are prepared to hand off the company and exit when you decide the time is right. Having a good strategy will enable your business legacy to continue long after you are no longer involved.

> *"Many of life's failures are people who did not realize how close they were to success when they gave up."*
> *—Thomas A. Edison*

Selling Your Business

Selling your business is a natural component of your exit strategy, but the decision to sell may not be easy. Most business owners have an emotional attachment to the business. Over the years they attract customers and develop friendships among them. They hire and train employees who look to them for their livelihood.

The time comes for every business owner to sell or transition the business to new owners. When the time comes, you want to make sure you do everything possible to:

- Protect the employees.
- Ensure a lasting business legacy.
- Provide the greatest value for the potential buyer.
- Secure the greatest possible sales price.

The best way to accomplish this is to secure the services of a trusted business broker. A good business broker will prove to be a valuable asset in the sale of your business.

Find a detailed outline at www.RealBusinessSolutionCenter.com/rbscresource center.

CHAPTER 16

Business Plans

Now that we have covered the basics, it is time to create a formal business plan. Are you ready?

This is the single most important item we will discuss. Remember our mantra: failing to plan means planning to fail.

This is the time to flesh out your business idea in greater detail, identify obstacles, helping to guarantee your your long-term success.

In addition to meeting the requirements of financial backers, you should have a written plan to help you clarify your business to your partners, employees, and—most important—yourself. Writing your plan can help you identify specific goals and objectives and understand possible threats to your business so you can address them early in the process.

When completing your business plan, you should be as specific as possible about the kind of business you are starting. Describe your business in terms of a mission statement or executive summary that clearly summarizes its purpose and is easily understood by you, your staff, potential investors, suppliers, and customers. Through this exercise you will assess the market, identify target customers, analyze your competition, develop a marketing strategy, and formulate a marketing plan.

- Who are your initial marketing targets?
- Why are you choosing these markets first?
- What products or services will you offer?

- Is there a specific volume or share of these markets that you hope to achieve?
- When do you hope to achieve these targets?
- Who will you target in the coming six months? In the coming year—or five to ten years?
- What methods will you use for each target segment?
- What specific actions will you take?
- Establish a timetable for each marketing activity.
- Determine the estimated costs of particular marketing activities.
- Determine how you will monitor and review progress.
- Determine how you will monitor and manage costs.
- Determine how you will handle the response to your marketing and re-adjust as needed.

You will need to describe your operations so you can make appropriate plans and estimate costs. Outline your plans for space, equipment, staff, suppliers, regulatory compliance, licensing, and so on.

Your business plan should include a breakdown of your financial requirements, the sources of financing you have available to you, and any additional amount that you may need. This breakdown should include:

- The cost of starting your business
- Details of your personal finances as well as additional financing
- A detailed cash flow forecast
- A profit and loss forecast
- Management team—Outline skills and experience.
- Key staff and responsibilities—Summarize roles and contribution to the business. Be sure to cover marketing and sales, financing, recruitment, product development, general management, distribution, and administration.
- Monitoring and coordination—Set out how you plan to monitor performance (against objectives and targets), and to coordinate the key roles in the business.
- Exit strategies

Your plan should include a realistic awareness of the risks involved, as well as how you plan to minimize them. Consider which of the following risks are relevant to your businesses:

- Lack of experience
- Economic uncertainties
- Reliance on a few key staff
- Reliance on a few suppliers
- Reliance on a small customer base
- Unpaid customer accounts
- Partnership difficulties
- Increased competition
- Theft and loss
- Failure to meet your targets

TIP: MAKE SURE YOU HAVE CONTINGENCY PLANS IN PLACE TO MINIMIZE RISK.

The following pages include a simple business plan that I use to help clients think through these critical components. Please take a few hours and complete the business plan in as much detail as possible. This exercise will help you flesh out all of the issues we have covered up to this point. Don't worry if it isn't perfect. This exercise is for *your* benefit. You can always come back and revise the draft as you have time to think through the issues and gather additional data.

I. Overview
  A. A good business plan helps define a goal.
    You cannot hit a target you cannot see. A business plan is essential if you need to raise outside capital. Even if you do not, it will help you focus on what is unique about your business and will give you an operational road map to follow.

  B. A business plan addresses three basic questions:
    - Where are we now?
    - Where do we want to go?
    - How will we get there?

C. A business plan:
- Provides a path to follow.
- Provides a tool to create a "statement of purpose" you can take to the bank, investor or buyer.
- Helps you think about competitive conditions, promotional opportunities, and situations that are advantageous to your business.

II. Develop Answers to These Questions:
  A. Why am I in business?
- To provide for my family
- To be my own boss
- To make money
- To control time and work hours
- To help people
- To serve the community
- To have business for my own use

_____

_____

_____

_____

_____

_____

_____

B. What business am I in?
Many business owners have difficulty because they are confused about this. You can't be everything to everybody. Answer the following questions:

- Do I have passion for the business?
- What is my value proposition?
- What is my niche? (Chapter 10 – Reread if you need to)
- Who is my perfect customer?
- What services do my customers ask for?
- Do I offer those services?
- What are my basic services and products?

C. What is my business plan?
The key components of a plan are:

- Description of the business
- The market
- Management and personnel
- Ownership structure
- Financial data and plans
- Operational plans
- Exit strategy

III. Developing a Business Plan
A. Description of Your Business
1. Describe your business.

_____

_____

_____

_____

_____

_____

_____

_____

2. **Name of Business**
   Do you need to file a business name? Call the license division of your secretary of state to check on the availability of a name. If you form a corporation, this check will be completed as part of the process. You can also conduct research via the Internet (www.switchboard.com and Google are good places to start).

   You can trademark your business name in most states. You can also secure a national trademark. If you plan on doing business outside of your home state, it is a good idea to do that. You can go directly to the United States Patent and Trademark Office to check on national availability of any name: www.uspto.gov.

3. **Brief History**
   If you are just starting your business, describe how and why you came up with this idea.

   _____

   _____

   _____

   _____

   _____

   _____

   _____

   _____

   _____

   _____

   _____

4. **Value Proposition**

   What value will your products or service bring to the market? Remember, you only have to do something 10 percent better or provide added value to be successful.

   _____

   _____

   _____

   _____

   _____

   _____

   _____

5. **Hours of Operation**

   Keep in mind you must make it easy for your customers. When are they most likely to shop?

   _____

   _____

   _____

   _____

   _____

   _____

6. **Customers' Perspective**
   How will your customers view your business? If you don't know, ask them. If you don't have customers yet, ask your friends and relatives.

   _____

   _____

   _____

   _____

   _____

   _____

7. **Strengths**
   What are your business's six greatest strengths? Don't just think of your Value Proposition what are the other things you do extremely well? Examples might include: prompt phone reply, twenty-four-hour delivery, wide selection of products, results, free shipping, money-back guarantee, etc.

   _____

   _____

   _____

   _____

   _____

   _____

_____

_____

_____

_____

_____

_____

_____

_____

_____

8. Challenges
What are your business's six greatest challenges?

_____

_____

_____

_____

_____

_____

_____

_____

_____

_____

_____

_____

_____

_____

_____

9. **Future Goals**
   Where do I want to be five years from now?

_____

_____

_____

_____

_____

_____

_____

_____

Will I need to expand or change services and space, or purchase equipment?

_____

_____

_____

_____

_____

_____

_____

_____

B. The Market (Determining Who Your Perfect Customer Is)
   1. What type of business do I have? What product or service will I provide?

_____

_____

_____

_____

_____

_____

_____

_____

2. **Describe my market:**
   Surprisingly, many business owners fail to do this. Understanding the current market is key to the success of any start-up company!

   _____

   _____

   _____

   _____

   _____

   _____

   _____

3. **Outline the demographics of my market (size, location, age, geographic area, etc.).**

   _____

   _____

   _____

   _____

   _____

   _____

   _____

4. Outline the characteristics of my customers (income level, age, social status, etc.).

_____

_____

_____

_____

_____

_____

_____

5. What is my position in the marketplace?
   a. Who are my competitors? How many of them are profitable?

_____

_____

_____

_____

_____

_____

_____

b. Do they have any advantages over me? Pricing, location, reputation?

_____

_____

_____

_____

_____

_____

_____

c. How many similar businesses went out of business in the past three years?

_____

_____

_____

_____

_____

_____

_____

d. How many similar businesses have opened?

_____

_____

_____

_____

_____

_____

_____

_____

6. Do I have a niche market?

_____

_____

_____

_____

_____

_____

_____

_____

7. **What tactics will I use to reach my perfect customer?**

_____

_____

_____

_____

_____

_____

_____

8. **What type of customers do I want? Is it more important to keep current customers or attract new ones? How can I convert prospects into customers? Will I have repeat sales to the same customers, or will I need new clients each time?**

_____

_____

_____

_____

_____

_____

_____

9. **How am I marketing to attract new customers and achieve top-of-mind awareness?**

_____

_____

_____

_____

_____

_____

_____

10. **Should I be going after new markets?**

_____

_____

_____

_____

_____

_____

_____

C. Management and Personnel

1. What does my organizational chart look like?

_____

_____

_____

_____

_____

_____

_____

2. What is my role as the owner/manager?

_____

_____

_____

_____

_____

_____

_____

3. **Will I need to hire employees? If so, what are their roles? Should I outsource certain functions?**

_____

_____

_____

_____

_____

_____

_____

_____

4. **What staff qualifications, training, and compensation will I need?**

_____

_____

_____

_____

_____

_____

_____

_____

5. **Are my job descriptions and expectations clear? Who does what, where, how, and when?**

_____

_____

_____

_____

_____

_____

6. **How do I recruit new staff members? What do I need to look for?**

_____

_____

_____

_____

_____

_____

7. **How will staff be involved in setting goals and visions of the business?**

_____

_____

_____

_____

_____

_____

_____

_____

D. **Ownership Structure**
    1. **Will I operate as a sole proprietor, LLC, S corporation, or C corporation?**

_____

_____

_____

_____

_____

_____

_____

2. **If I form a partnership, who will make decisions? Is there a management agreement or contract? Do we agree on core values? How will business assets be distributed in the event the partnership is dissolved?**

    _____

    _____

    _____

    _____

    _____

    _____

    _____

3. **What would happen if I were no longer around?**

    _____

    _____

    _____

    _____

    _____

    _____

4. What is my business worth?

Even if your business is just starting out, you need to estimate the value.

_____

_____

_____

_____

_____

_____

_____

5. Do I have an exit strategy?

If you died, what would happen to your business? If your partner decides to leave next year, what would happen to his/her ownership share? How would you determine a value?

_____

_____

_____

_____

_____

_____

_____

_____

E. Financial Data and Plans

1. **How is money generated? Is there just one source of revenue, or can I identify multiple streams of income (walk-in customers, Internet sales, direct mail marketing, trade fairs, and corporate purchases)?**

   _____

   _____

   _____

   _____

   _____

   _____

   _____

2. **What are the price options on goods or services?**
   Regarding payment options, have you implemented pay terms? A purchase order system? Contracts? Can you increase sales by providing additional pay term options without risking costly receivables, etc.?

   _____

   _____

   _____

   _____

   _____

   _____

   _____

3. **What new equipment will I need in the next three years (copiers, computers, lawn care, automotive)?**

_____

_____

_____

_____

_____

_____

_____

_____

4. **What is the anticipated revenue per customer or item sold?**

_____

_____

_____

_____

_____

_____

_____

_____

5. **Will I rent or purchase office and warehouse space for my business?**

_____

_____

_____

_____

_____

_____

_____

6. **Do I have a formal business budget? Have I established a process to monitor monthly sales goals?**
Take a moment to establish benchmarks and define what would have to happen each week to achieve those goals.

_____

_____

_____

_____

_____

_____

_____

7. **How do I estimate and control monthly cash flow? What is my break-even point? How much money do I have in a business savings account?**
    Put systems in place so you can monitor how income and expenses are doing.

    _____

    _____

    _____

    _____

    _____

    _____

    _____

8. **Who will maintain daily financial records?**
    Keep this as a priority. If you are not good at this, enlist the services of someone who is.

    _____

    _____

    _____

    _____

    _____

    _____

    _____

9. **How will I withdraw my own compensation?**
   Even with no employees, it's wise to have a payroll company or CPA issue paychecks. What they provide in keeping you current on taxes is invaluable.

   _____

   _____

   _____

   _____

   _____

   _____

   _____

10. **Should I buy or lease new equipment?**
    Look at these options with your accountant.

    _____

    _____

    _____

    _____

    _____

    _____

    _____

11. What options do I have for financing? How will I raise more money if I need to put more in before the business shows a profit?

_____

_____

_____

_____

_____

_____

_____

_____

12. What insurance, lease, rental, or consulting agreements need to be negotiated?

_____

_____

_____

_____

_____

_____

_____

_____

13. Have I sought wise counsel from my spouse, friends, pastor, or a business coach?

_____

_____

_____

_____

_____

_____

_____

14. What technology will I need to implement?

_____

_____

_____

_____

_____

_____

_____

15. Do I have the support of my spouse?

If the answer to this question is no, stop now and revisit the idea with your spouse. Without the support of your spouse, you will place undue strain on your marriage and business.

_____

_____

_____

_____

_____

_____

_____

By now you should have a strong understanding of your business, customer base, and marketing strategy. Before I leave this section, there is one more topic we should cover: comprehensive business plans.

Some of my clients have said that they really like the simple business plan, but the lending agency won't accept what they have prepared because the agency insists on a more detailed version.

This is a reality.

While the simple version above is all you will ever need to organize your business, most lending agencies expect to see a far more comprehensive business plan before they will issue the loan. They expect to see additional detail related to location and demographics at a minimum.

The same is true when seeking venture capital.

I have included a comprehensive business planning guide in the resource section at the back of the book. If you need to establish a business plan for a loan, the comprehensive plan is the one you should use.

CHAPTER 17

Setting Up the Business

Now you are ready to establish your business, but there are several procedural items that you will need to address. These are in no particular order but must be completed prior to opening your business.

Business Name

First, decide on a good business name. This is a matter of personal preference. The thing to remember is that you will be building a brand under your chosen name. Many business owners will use their last name (Smith & Associates) while others prefer to remain somewhat anonymous. If you are building a consulting business, I would recommend using your personal name. This will help as you seek out opportunities to speak and grow your business.

Once you have narrowed the selection down (not more than two or three), research each one carefully. Do a Google search on each name to see what pops up. Check to see if the domain name has already been purchased by someone else. If so, it will severely limit your ability to use that name in your website or blog.

Business Logo

While certainly important, this is not a deal breaker. You want to choose a meaningful logo that people will immediately associate with your company. The branding process typically evolves over time, but you need a logo early in the process. A good example is the Nike logo. It does not include the name *Nike* anywhere on the logo, but every time someone sees it, they immediately think of Nike.

The key is not to spend a lot of money on a logo design. There are several resources available for just a few hundred dollars.

Articles of Incorporation

If you decide to create a corporation, nonprofit, limited liability company, or partnership (limited or limited liability), you will need to register your business and file certain documents with your state. If your business is a sole proprietorship, you do not need to register your business with the state.

Note: Many states require a sole proprietor to use his or her own name for the business name unless the person formally files another name as a trade name, or a DBA (doing business as) name.

Use the SBA website to see what is required in your state: www.sba.gov/category/navigation-structure/starting-managing-business/starting-business/establishing-business/incorporating-registering-your-.

Tax ID

If you plan to operate as a sole proprietor, your tax ID is typically your social security number.

If you plan to set up a partnership, LLC, or corporation, you will need to secure an Employer Identification Number (EIN). An EIN is also known as a Federal Tax Identification Number and is used to identify a business entity. Generally, businesses need an EIN. You may apply for an EIN in various ways. Use the IRS website for specific details: www.irs.gov/businesses/small/article/0,,id=99021,00.html.

Tax Requirements

Sales Tax—Now identify how and where to pay your business sales tax, if applicable.

In addition to your federal business taxes, you are required to pay state and local sales tax (city, county, and state) if you are selling a tangible item. Each state and locality has its own tax laws. You should contact the revenue office for each to see what is required in your area.

In most states, business owners are required to register their businesses with a state tax agency and apply for certain tax permits. For example, in order to collect sales tax from customers, many states require businesses to apply for a state sales tax permit.

Income Tax—Nearly every state levies a business or corporate income tax. Your tax requirement depends on the structure of your business. As an example, if your business is operating as an LLC, the LLC will be taxed independent from the owners. Sole proprietors report their personal and business income tax together using specific forms. Consult a local CPA to obtain specific requirements for your business classification.

Employment Tax—In addition to federal employment taxes, business owners with employees are responsible for paying certain taxes required by the state. All states require payment of state workers' compensation insurance and unemployment insurance taxes. Certain states (currently California, Hawaii, New Jersey, New York, and Rhode Island) and Puerto Rico require businesses to pay for temporary disability insurance.

Visit the SBA website to determine what is required in your state: www. sba.gov/category/navigation-structure/starting-managing-business/ starting-business/establishing-business/taxes.

Business License

When you open your business, you will also need to secure a business license. There are a few exceptions to this rule, so check with your state to see if your business falls under an existing exception.

As a general rule, every business needs one or more federal, state, or local licenses or permits to operate. Licenses can range from a basic operating license to very specific permits.

Regulations vary by industry, state, and locality, so it's very important to understand the licensing rules where your business is located. Not complying with licensing and permitting regulations can lead to expensive fines and put your business at serious risk.

Visit the SBA website to see what permits are required in your area: www.sba.gov/content/search-business-licenses-and-permits

CHAPTER 18

Conclusion

Can you believe we are almost through?

I hope this book has opened your eyes to some of the complexities of business as well as the opportunities that await you.

There are many steps along the path to business success, but taking the time to understand is the most important step you will ever take.

Once you have determined your skills and abilities, you are in a position to stretch your imagination.

I learn more about business and myself every day. I would love to hear how this information has helped you succeed in your business venture, and we encourage you to become a member of the Real Business Solution Center community. You can always reach us via the Contact Us link at www. RealBusinessSolutionCenter.com. If you have questions as you develop and grow your business, please let me know by posting questions and comments to the discussion forum on our site.

I want to leave you with a brief outline of my personal coaching strategy. I have used this strategy successfully throughout the years. I call it the RBSC Advantage. Take some time to answer each question until you are certain everything is in place.

I wish you the best of success in your pursuit of business excellence!

> *"Success usually comes to those who are too busy to be looking for it."*
> —Henry David Thoreau

RBSC Advantage

Step 1—The Sphere of Excellence

The foundation for the RBSC Advantage is the Sphere of Excellence. These five simple strategies will help you stay on the right path.

RBSC Sphere of Excellence

1. Planning—Establish a plan and revisit it often.
2. Education and Training—Seek out any needed training.
3. Value Proposition—Forge a strong value proposition.
4. Capital—Make sure you have the funding required.
5. Coaching/Mentoring—Secure wise counsel.

Step 2—Feasibility Checklist

This feasibility checklist is designed to help the prospective businessperson determine whether his or her idea represents a valid business opportunity. The high failure rate of new businesses indicates that relatively few new businesses result in successful ventures. That is because too many entrepreneurs strike out on a business venture absolutely convinced of its merits without having adequately evaluated its real potential.

1. Do you enjoy working long hours?
2. Do you have self-discipline and willpower?
3. Do you meet deadlines easily?
4. Do you work well under stress?
5. Will you jeopardize your home?
6. Do you have the necessary physical strength?
7. Does your family support this venture?
8. Do you have a backup plan?

Experience and Skill

1. Does your idea make use of your skills?
2. Does your idea require skills you do not have?
3. Can you find experienced personnel at an affordable rate?
4. Are you experienced in this line of work?
5. Do you have managerial experience?
6. Are you able to interpret financial data?
7. Are you familiar with tax regulations?
8. Do you know bookkeeping and accounting?

Planning and Preparedness

1. Have you already written a formal business plan?
2. Do you know exactly what services or products will be offered?
3. Do you know what customers to target?
4. Have you arranged for a business location?
5. Do you have a list of potential suppliers?

6. Do you know your competitors' businesses well?
7. Have you arranged for insurance?
8. Do you have a business license?
9. Have you investigated advertising and its cost?
10. Have you hired a competent staff?

Requirements for Success

1. Will your proposed business meet unserved needs?
2. Is there already a similar business in your community?
3. Can your business successfully compete against the competition because of an advantage such as lower prices or superior service?

Detrimental Flaws

1. Are you affected by any monopolies, shortages, or restrictions that prevent you from obtaining any necessary items at an affordable price?
2. Are capital requirements for starting up or continuing operations excessive?
3. Is adequate financing going to be difficult to obtain?
4. Does your business adversely affect the environment?
5. Is your business completely legal?
6. Are there any factors that prevent effective marketing?

Income

1. Will your business provide you with your desired level of income?
2. Do you know your industry's averages, including gross profit, expenses, and net profit as a percent of sales?
3. Do you know your industry's inventory turnover rate?
4. Have you prepared an income statement to determine the level of sales necessary to support your desired income level?
5. From a practical standpoint, can you support the level of sales in question 4?

This checklist is a tool to help the entrepreneur determine if there are any major obstacles that will prevent the business from becoming successful. Each *no* answer should be carefully reviewed to determine how great an impact it will have on the business and to see if anything can be done to correct the problems it may create.

Step 3—Readiness Checklist

The readiness checklist enables entrepreneurs to walk through a series of questions designed to identify areas they may have missed in their initial planning phase.

1.   Have you decided on a location?
2.   Have you found a good building?
3.   Is it big enough to allow for growth?
4.   Can people get to it easily?
5.   Do you have adequate parking available?
6.   Do you have a proper sign?
7.   Have you signed the necessary papers?
8.   Has a lawyer checked the lease and zoning?
9.   Are the utilities in line?

Equipment and Office Supplies

1.   Do you have the necessary office equipment?
2.   Do you have a reliable source?
3.   Can you afford to maintain proper levels of supplies and the upkeep of equipment?

Your Merchandise

1.   Do you know precisely what will be sold?
2.   Are you qualified to sell it?
3.   Can you afford the suppliers' prices?
4.   Can the supplier provide the services you need?
5.   Do you know how to merchandise your goods?
6.   Do you have the necessary inventory?

Record Keeping

1.   Have you planned a system of records for income, expenses, etc.?
2.   Have you worked out an effective inventory tracking system?

3. Do you know how to keep payroll, tax, and payment records?
4. Do you know what financial statements will be needed?
5. Do you have an accountant, if one is needed?

Legal Records

1. Do you have all the necessary licenses and permits?
2. Do you know what business laws you have to obey?
3. Do you have a lawyer with small business expertise?

Protection

1. Have you made plans for protecting against both employee and customer theft?
2. Have you talked with an insurance agent about all the kinds of insurance you need?

Advertising

1. Do you have a marketing plan?
2. Do you know how you will advertise?
3. Can you afford adequate advertising?

Pricing

1. Do you know the selling price for each item to be sold?
2. Do you know your competitors' prices?
3. Can you make a profit with the prices at which you intend to sell?
4. Do you have a pricing strategy for old merchandise or slow-to-sell merchandise?

Buying

1. Do you have a plan for determining what your customers want?
2. Is it both workable and affordable?
3. Do you have buying experience?
4. Do you have reliable suppliers?

Selling

1. Do you have a selling strategy?
2. Can you afford the necessary staffing?
3. Do you have a plan flexible enough to cover both the slow and peak times?
4. Are you and your employees experienced in selling?

Employees

1. Have you hired the necessary staff?
2. Do your staff members have the needed experience?
3. Have you set personnel procedures?
4. Do you have a benefits package?
5. Do you have a performance appraisal system?
6. Do you have a training program and procedure manuals for new employees?
7. Do you have an employee recruitment plan?
8. Can you offer employees insurance coverage?
9. Do you know what the total salaries and benefits will equal?
10. Can you afford this figure?

Credit

1. Will your customers have the option of buying on credit?
2. Have you arranged for the use of credit cards?
3. Do you have a method for determining good creditors from the risky ones?
4. Have you set credit acceptance procedures for the staff to follow?

Other

1. Could you make more money working for someone else?
2. Can you afford the loss if the business fails?
3. Do you have a plan to repay debts?
4. Does your family support you completely?
5. Do you have the energy and time to run a business?

6. Do you have adequate funding?
7. Will you need to mortgage your home or use it as collateral? (Not recommended for your families security)
8. Do you have managerial experience in each aspect of your business?

This checklist is an important tool in the planning of your new business. Each of these areas must be addressed by the entrepreneur. By following this checklist, the business owner can deal with many of the problems that face a new venture before they become major obstacles.

Serious consideration should be given to the viability of the venture if the entrepreneur has many questions that cannot be addressed or rectified.

Step 4—Stay True to Your Business Plan

Follow your plan, revisit the plan often, and make adjustments as needed. Remember, this is your road map to success!

"It's a curious old world, son. Hang on and enjoy the ride."
—Harold Justice (my grandfather)

BONUS CHAPTER

Biblical Principles of Business

I am far from a theologian, but I am a man of faith. I believe the Bible teaches us many things about life and business. I would like to leave you with a few simple guides that I have found helpful throughout my life and career. I hope you find them to be as valuable as I have.

Mental and Spiritual Preparedness

One of life's greatest journeys is spiritual. In order to fully achieve the satisfaction of your business venture, you must first be prepared mentally and spiritually.

I recommend the following reading to help you reach your optimal goal.

When you are:	Read:
Discouraged	Isaiah 51:11, Proverbs 1:69, and Galatians 6:9
Worried	I Peter 5:7, Philippians 4:6–7, and Isaiah 26:3
Lonely	Isaiah 41:10, John 14:18, and Deuteronomy 33:27
Depressed	Psalm 30:5, Isaiah 40:31, and Corinthians 1:3–4
Confused	I Corinthians 14:33, James 1:5, and Proverbs 3:5–6
Angry	James 1:19–20, Ephesians 4:26, and Proverbs 15:1
Tempted	I Corinthians 10:12–13, Psalm 119:11, and I Peter 5:8–9
Afraid	John 14:27, II Timothy 1:7, and Psalm 56:11
Grieving	Psalm 23, Psalm 147:3, and Hebrew 4:15–16
Troubled	Nahum 1:7, Psalm 4:8, and Psalm 138:7
Deserted	Psalm 9:10, Psalm 27:10, and Romans 8:38–39

The above passages can be found in any Bible; however, I recommend the New International Version (NIV) for ease of reading.

> *"Our help is in the name of the Lord, who made heaven and earth." (Psalm 124:8)*

What people need to be encouraged about most frequently:

1. *The length of time it requires to find a new job or start a new business.* Passion and planning can make you successful, but expect it to take some time (résumés, networking, career planning, business planning, coaching, etc.).
2. *Elevator speech.* You must be able to articulate who you are, what you do, and why you are an expert in your field (practice this over and over in the mirror so it comes across believable and smooth).
3. *Understanding the sales process/interview process.* People generally know why they want a specific job or why they want to go into business. Unfortunately most prospective employers and customers are unmotivated by your needs and desires. You must help them understand how you or your company will benefit them. Learn how to approach an interview or a sales call. (Perspective is everything, and perception feeds perspective.)
4. *Negotiating.* If you take a position with a company, you may be required to negotiate your salary and benefits during the interview process. Once you are hired, you will need to negotiate personalities with coworkers and assigned duties. (There are people with titles who have power over your work, and there are others who have the power to influence. Figure out who's who and act accordingly.)
5. *Maintaining a long-term perspective.* You are living out God's purpose, and that purpose may vary from time to time. It may even feel like you're taking a step sideways or even backward from time to time. Pray about the situation and take action. Step out and do what you feel called to do. (We all have seasons of growing.)

Honesty and Integrity

The Bible compels us to conduct business in an upright and honest manner.

Proverbs 3:32 says, "For the crooked man is an abomination to the Lord; but He is intimate with the upright."

Another key verse is found in Proverbs 4:24: "Put away from you a deceitful mouth, and put devious lips far from you."

In simple terms we as business owners should strive to always treat our customers fairly. That can mean fair pricing, not cutting corners, or honoring your word. Provide quality products and services at a fair price. Honor your debts and treat everyone with the respect you desire for yourself.

Wise Counsel

We have already covered the benefits of wise counsel in an earlier chapter, but I want to leave you with a strong foundation in this area.

Proverbs 14:15 says, "The naïve believes everything, but the prudent man considers his steps."

Proverbs 15:22 says, "Without consultation, plans are frustrated, but with many counselors they succeed."

Always seek out wise counsel. This can mean the difference between a successful or a failed business.

That doesn't mean you should try to find someone who will agree with your position, or a consultant who will render a formal recommendation to support your idea. Likewise, you shouldn't stop when you find someone who agrees with you. Always seek counsel from multiple sources!

Seeking wise counsel means you are humbled before God seeking his will and direction in your business decision. Wise counsel can come from a spouse, friend, pastor, customer, networking group, or business coach.

I always run business decisions by my spouse. It is my belief that God provided her to be my helpmate. She helps to keep me grounded and focused on the task at hand. If you don't have the support of your spouse, you should walk away from business opportunities.

Employees

How do you choose the right employee?

The first step is to clearly define the job you want them to do. People will always perform best when they know what the rules are. Make sure you have a well-defined personnel manual outlining:

- The scope and responsibility of each position
- The process for hiring and firing employees, job standards (time, dress code, lunch, breaks, socializing during work hours, cell phone usage, smoking, drinking, expected output, and gossip).

When interviewing for a position, choose the candidate that is best suited for not only the position but the environment as well.

Proverbs 22:29 says, "Do you see a man skilled in his work? He will stand before kings; he will not stand before obscure men."

Use a good personality profile to help isolate each candidate's personality type. Review the results and choose a group of candidates who are best aligned with your core business values and best suited for the business environment. Then select the candidate with the credentials best suited to perform the duties you have outlined.

Implement a trial period for employment. I generally recommend a six-month trial period during which the employee can be terminated without cause.

Never allow race, gender, or age to enter into the equation. Over my thirty-year career, I have found that having a good mix of race, gender, and age creates a healthy work environment.

Finally, treat your employees with respect and honor, even when you have to help them off the bus!

Payroll

How do you set the pay scale for your employees?

James 5:4 says, "Behold, the pay of the laborers who moved your fields, and which has been withheld by you, cries out against you; and the outcry of those who did the harvesting has reached the ears of the Lord of Sabaoth."

This verse does not compel us to pay everyone the same wage. Those who do more work should be paid a higher wage.

This verse does, however, compel us to pay employees for the work they have completed at the wage they agreed to work for. We should never try to cheat our employees out of wages they are due.

As a Christian manager, I believe we have a responsibility to meet the minimum needs of any employee. Notice I said *needs* as opposed to *wants* and *desires*. This is a critical distinction. We need to pay a wage that will enable employees to provide suitable food, clothing, shelter, and transportation for their families.

Summary:

- Never withhold wages.
- Reward employees for service above and beyond the call of duty.
- Reward loyalty (never lay off an older worker merely to lower your salary expense).
- Always provide a wage that will allow the employee to meet the minimum needs of his or her family.
- Treat all employees with respect and honor.

Is borrowing biblical?

I have had clients ask whether borrowing is biblical.

Scripture tells us that everything we have belongs to God. We are merely the stewards to whom He has entrusted certain money and possessions.

The scripture contains plenty of verses related to the foolishness of guaranteeing the debts of others (surety), becoming slave to the lender, etc.

Romans 13:8 even goes so far as to say, "owe no one anything."

At first that sounds like a prohibition against any sort of borrowing; however, when taken in the full context of Romans 13:8, the word *owe* appears to refer only to current obligations.

For example, if we don't pay our taxes when due, then we owe and have not met our obligations.

This same principle applies to your business assets. When you assume a loan, you have created a future obligation to make monthly payments. I believe this passage is exhorting us to meet all of our proper obligations on time.

Though borrowing in itself may be allowable, it does come with inherent risk. If you assume a business loan, make sure you have fully analyzed the risk.

Luke 16:13 says, "No servant can serve two masters; for either he will hate the one, and love the other, or else he will hold to one, and despise the other. You cannot serve God and mammon."

The key here is to always keep God first in your business dealings. If you put your business and money ahead of God, you will lack balance. How do you know when you stray? Some of the more common symptoms include:

- Working longer hours
- Spending more time away from family
- Possessing conceit and arrogance; lacking humility
- Assuming unnecessary debt; taking out excessive loans
- Looking for easy money and get-rich-quick opportunities
- Cheating customers

> *"Whether, then, you eat or drink or whatever you do, do all for the glory of God." (1 Corinthians 10:31)*

Partnerships

Business owners are faced with a multitude of decisions. In fact, one of the more critical decisions takes place before the business ever takes off. "Should I take on a partner?"

The Bible paints a powerful illustration in 2 Corinthians 6:14, which states believers should not be yoked (or bound) together with nonbelievers. While this verse pertains to marriage, the obvious logic behind the apostle's admonition is that we shouldn't enter into business with anyone of unequal values.

It has been my experience that many who call themselves Christians are no more ethical than non-Christians when it comes to conducting business. Although, as Christians we should strive to stand apart.

When entering into a partnership, it is critical to ask two questions: 1) Who will be in charge? and 2) Do we agree on core values?

Here are a few simple questions that you should ask prior to entering into any partnership:

- Will we give to the church, missions, and charity?
- Are we willing to sue customers or suppliers over a dispute?
- Will we allow family members to work for the company?
- Will we employ anyone who is not a Christian?
- How much time will we commit to travel away from family?
- How many hours per week will we work?
- How many hours per week will we spend in the office?
- Who will be in charge?
- How will business assets be distributed in the event we dissolve the partnership?
- Have we agreed on a formal business plan?

At the end of the day, people are people whether they are Christians or not. It is always best to have open and honest discussions up front, and then have a formal agreement drafted to cover the understanding between the partners. Even the best of friends or family can turn when conflict arises!

Note: An obvious exception to this rule is when your spouse is your business partner.

Assuming both parties are equally yoked and have agreed on core values, I find no biblical principle that would otherwise forbid the forming of a partnership.

Charity

Should I tithe from my business income?

Tithing is a very personal action. It is an outward demonstration of our faith and appreciation for the blessings God has placed in our lives. In 2 Corinthians 9:7 it says, "Let each one do just as he has purposed in his heart; not grudgingly or under compulsion; for God loves a cheerful giver."

Proverbs 3:9 says, "Honor the Lord from your wealth and from the first of all your produce."

I personally tithe on my gross personal income, or, in other words, my first fruits.

Others have told me they tithe on the business profits as well.

The Bible teaches that we are to give our tithe to the storehouse with additional offerings going toward charity. While this issue is heavily debated between New Testament Christians and Old Testament Christians, tithe is generally defined as 10 percent of our first fruits and the storehouse as the church and missions.

The key is this: Only you can decide. This is a personal commitment between you and God!

Life Map

The following is a guide to help you on your spiritual journey. It will show you that there is an easy way to know the Lord Jesus Christ as your personal savior and to know for sure that when you die you will go to heaven.

Step 1—Realize That God Loves You

"For God so loved the world that he gave his only begotten son, that whosoever believeth in him should not perish, but have everlasting life." (John 3:16)

The Bible tells us that all men are sinners. It is our sin that has separated us from God. "For all have sinned and come short of the glory of God." (Romans 3:23)

God made man in his own image and gave him the ability to choose right from wrong. We choose to sin, and this is what separates us from God.

The Bible also tells us that sin must be paid for. "For the wages of sin are death…" (Romans 6:23)

The payment for sin is death and eternal separation from God. If we continue to sin, we will die without Christ and will be separated from God forever.

The good news is that Christ paid for our sin. "But God commendeth his love toward us, in that, while we were yet sinners Christ died for us." (Romans 5:8)

All of our sins were laid on Christ when he was placed on the cross. He died on the cross, paid our sin debt, and arose again.

Step 2—Personally Pray and Receive Christ into Your life

"For whosoever shall call upon the name of the Lord shall be saved." (Romans 10:13)

That's right, simply pray to receive Christ, and receive him by faith.

Pray today to receive Christ: "Lord, I know I am a sinner. If I died today, I would not go to heaven. Forgive my sins, and come into my life to be my savior. Help me to live for you from this day forward. In Jesus's name I pray. Amen."

Step 3—Live Your New Christian Life

Everlasting life begins when you receive Christ into your life. Take this gift and let Christ be your guide as you enjoy all of life's fantastic journeys.

RESOURCES

Web Resources

www.RealBusinessSolutionCenter.com

Recommended Reading List

I have read hundreds of business books over the span of my career, and I have noted many of them throughout this book. While I won't list them all, I would like to provide you with a list I consider to be the best on the market. All are available from Amazon.

Business By The Book by Larry Burkett
The Answer by John Assaraf and Murray Smith
Good to Great by Jim Collins
QBQ! The Question Behind the Question by John G. Miller
The 7 Habits of Highly Effective People by Stephen R. Covey
Guerrilla Marketing by Jay Conrad Levinson
Raving Fans by Ken Blanchard and Sheldon Bowles
The One Minute Manager by Kenneth H. Blanchard and Spencer Johnson
Flipping the Switch by John G. Miller
Guerrilla Marketing for Consultants by Jay Conrad Levinson and Michael W. McLaughlin
Built to Last by Jim Collins and Jerry I. Porras
One Man's Full Life by Earl E. Bakken
The E-Myth Revisited by Michael E. Gerber
Get Rich Click! by Marc Ostrofsky
SPIN Selling by Neil Rackham
Major Account Sales Strategy by Neil Rackham
Become a Coach by Justin Lukasavige

48 Days to the Work You Love by Dan Miller
The Power of Respect by Deborah Norville
Financial Peace Revisited by Dave Ramsey

A complete listing can be found at http://astore.amazon.com/keystfinancon-20.

Top Fifty Business Tips

I asked a group of business owners for the top three business tips they would recommend to someone starting out. The following list contains their responses. There are obviously more than three on the list, but I want you to have the benefit of them all.

1. Take time to explore and understand whether running your own business is right for you. You may find that you are not compatible.
2. Pick your niche. Take stock of your skills, interests, and employment history to select the business that is best suited for you.
3. Create your business plan. The exercise of creating a business plan is what pays the dividends.
4. When starting a business, there are three key building blocks. The first building block is passion, which is key to the success of any new business. The second building block is planning (failing to plan means planning to fail). The third building block is value. Passion and planning are essential to any successful business, but without value they too will struggle.
5. Create a value proposition that sets you apart from your competitors. If your competitors can say the same thing about their company, then you aren't adding value and that will force you to compete on price.
6. Employ the power of positive quitting. When you quit all the things that aren't working for you, and when you stop tolerating the negative things that hold you back, you create a positive flow in your business.
7. Identify areas where you are the weakest and the resources you will employ to manage those aspects of the business. Surround yourself with people who are knowledgeable in areas that you aren't.

8. Seek help from small business peers, a mentor, business coach, or trade association. They can help you overcome some of the trial and error of beginning your business.

9. Do not automatically assume you need bankers and investors at the outset of your business.

10. Get your personal finances in order before you jump into the entrepreneurship world. Always protect the basic needs of your family!

11. Speak with your CPA and determine which business structure is right for you (sole proprietorship, LLC, S corp, etc.).

12. Secure the appropriate business license and register your business.

13. Secure insurance to minimize risk.

14. Establish a web presence. Create a website and begin to interact with social media.

15. Businesses compete in three ways: quality, service, and price. You typically get to pick two of the three, but not all. Most small businesses need to compete on quality and service.

16. Take time to determine the key characteristics of your perfect customer (80 percent of your sales will come from 20 percent of your customers).

17. When it comes to marketing, you have to find your niche, the product or service your company will provide to your perfect customer.

18. Establish a marketing strategy. A well-defined marketing strategy involves three elements: where, what, and how. Remember, nothing happens until a sale is made. You need a good marketing plan to sell your product or service.

19. Determine which distribution channel is right for your business.

20. No matter how busy you are, spend at least 25 percent of your time with customers. You cannot make the proper business decision without understanding their viewpoint.

21. The best way to satisfy your customers is not by selling them products but by giving solutions to their problems.

22. Quality takes minutes to lose but years to regain. In small businesses, profitability must come first but not at the sacrifice of quality.

23. Vendors are partners too! Treat your vendors like customers.

24. Invest in understanding tax issues that affect your small business or hire a CPA.

25. Whatever happens to a small business happens at the hands of the people who work for it.

26. Network, network, network.
27. Write a business plan with measurable goals, expenses, and expectations that includes a lot of "what if?" statements (both bad and good). What if my costs double? What if income is slow to come in? What if a supplier goes out of business? What if sales take off? How do I grow faster than planned?
28. Find a niche (what makes you different from the rest).
29. Have an exit strategy. No matter how much you may think you love what you will be doing, you need to know how you will get out.
30. Make sure that you have adequate capital, or financing, available for the business. A common mistake businesses make is underestimating the capital necessary for a business.
31. Do your homework and know about your market, prospective customers, and the competition.
32. Have some knowledge of the business you want to pursue.
33. Research and talk to anyone and everyone you can about this business. Regroup and rewrite your business plan until it will work.
34. Raise enough money so that under most circumstances, should you fail, you will not bankrupt yourself.
35. Start something you *really* enjoy and feel passionate about. It's always challenging starting any business, but if you love what you're trying to do, it'll help you through the tougher days as you get your footing.
36. Test and tweak.
37. On day one start entering contacts into a contact management system. Start using simple segmentation and build upon it as you learn more about customers, prospects, suppliers, and even the competition. Treat the list of contacts as an asset. As the business evolves, your marketing strategy will keep you on a path of growth.
38. You cannot ever have enough information about your marketplace.
39. Always keep your income opportunities open. When we keep our minds open, we may discover a good product line that would marry well with what we carry, or a partnership with someone that might be beneficial. Stay open to all income opportunities.
40. Have enough money saved on the personal side. It gives you freedom to be more selective of your clientele. It's easier to serve one great client than ten mediocre ones.
41. Get help as soon as possible—whether it is employees, legal, professional, etc. Starting with a good base is important so you don't run

into problems early that will derail your company's growth and/or future.

42. Do a very simple flowchart of how a customer enters and leaves your company (how the transaction takes place). From there decide what steps add value to the transaction. Once identified, farm out any task that is better handled by a lower paid employee. Discontinue tasks that provide no value.

43. Get over yourself! A pitfall that most self-employed folks fall in is that they think they are the only ones who can do the job (and that no one can do it better), which is never true. Your goal is to build a business that gives you the time and money to pursue the reason you actually started your own business—having more time with family, being your own boss, etc.

44. Survive for six months with no income. Find a client/customer to get you started (preferably before you actually launch the business). Sell, sell, sell.

45. If two or more individuals are opening a business together, regardless of whether it is a partnership, corporation, or other legal entity, there should be a clear and detailed agreement. The agreement should state how the business will be operated, who will make decisions, and how profits/losses will split. It is always better to discuss these issues prior to opening the business while everyone still likes each other.

46. Know who your ideal client is inside and out. Without knowing who you are marketing toward, you're not talking to anyone specific and are diffusing your efforts.

47. Create a brand that speaks directly to that ideal client—including logo, website, and other marketing materials—to ensure your actions match that brand!

48. Create an effective marketing campaign to promote your niche to your targeted audience.

49. Use any and all communication channels that are relevant to your business.

50. Go to free courses (if available in your area). Learn about different aspects of business and network. Be cautious about free courses. There are accidental experts out there who give the impression they know what they're talking about but really don't or don't have the knowledge and expertise to know the bigger picture. You really have to choose wisely whom you are going to learn from and ensure they have the credentials to back up their teachings.

Comprehensive Business Plan

This guide was written for you, the owner/manager of an emerging business. It is divided into several components: goal setting, company background, product/service description, personnel, marketing, and finance. It is designed to take you step by step through the process of preparing your business plan.

A well-conceived business plan is essential to the capital-raising process for your emerging company. It is an excellent way for an investor—whether a venture capitalist or other provider of funds—to review your company's potential. Today, many investors will not even consider meeting with you until they have read your business plan. And the quality of your plan can be a major factor in an investor's decision to help fund your venture.

A business plan is also a management tool. It can help focus, in a logical and organized manner, on the future growth of your company. It helps you to anticipate and meet the inevitable changes of the future. Further, a business plan is a control tool that permits you to monitor and assess progress.

I hope this guide assists your company in its planning process and provides the payback that a well-developed plan will bring. View it online at www.realbusinesssolutioncenter.com/resource-center/business-startconsulting.com/doc/Howtobusinessplan.doc.

Marketing Strategies

- Advertising (TV, Radio, Print)
- Affiliate
- Affinity marketing
- Barter
- Catalog marketing
- Direct marketing
- Event marketing
- Frequent-buyer program
- Internet
- Outdoor media
- Point of purchase (POP) and point of sale (POS)
- Promotions and cross-promotions

- Public relations (PR)
- Signage

Marketing Tactics

- Ad tracking
- AdSense (Google)
- Articles
- Auctions
- Audio marketing
- Autoresponders
- Banner ads
- Blogging
- Business cards
- Case studies
- Consulting
- Contests
- Discussion groups
- eBay
- E-books
- E-mail campaigns
- E-zines
- Feedback forms
- Forums
- Guarantees
- Info products
- Internet radio
- Interviews
- Keywords
- Mailing lists
- Membership sites
- Mini courses
- Ministries
- Network marketing
- Newsletters
- Pay-per-click
- Postcards

- Pricing
- Private label
- Public speaking
- SEO (search engine optimization)
- Seminars and workshops
- Surveys
- Teleseminars
- Testimonials
- Tips
- Toll-free number
- Tutorials
- Upsell
- Videos
- Web pages
- Yellow Pages

Common Sales Channel Examples

- Direct sales
- Events
- Mail order
- Online marketing
- Phone sales
- Retail

Value Proposition Examples

- Fix it right
- Fix it fast or on time (quick resolution)
- Honesty (only fix what is broken)
- Don't charge more than you agreed
- No hassles
- Low risk
- Price
- Free products or services
- Free education
- Quality workmanship

- Provide expected results, on time and at the cost stated. Provide additional options and variety.
- Customer service
- Guaranteed results
- No hassles
- Variety
- Follow-through
- Expected results
- Convenience

Finance and Budgeting Tools

The following RBSC Quickie Budget is an excellent guide for financial freedom in your business. Combined with the Financial Baby Steps for Business, the results can be tremendous.

Find additional financial tools at www.RealBusinessSolutionCenter.com/resource-center/financial-resources.

Forty Marketing Ideas

1. Lead a workshop through your local church, Chamber of Commerce, or civic group.
2. Start a free newsletter.
3. Create a twenty-, forty-, and sixty-minute presentation on your area of expertise.
4. Speak to a group two or three times a month.
5. Send an op-ed piece to your local newspaper or business publication.
6. Submit an article to thirty different magazines and newspapers.
7. Send out press releases.
8. Do something newsworthy.
9. Give away a one-hundred-point checklist for health in your area of expertise.
10. Give away free audio CDs on your specialty. Tell people everything you know about achieving success in that area.
11. Develop an intake information form.
12. Offer to help someone in the news who could use your help.
13. Be an expert on a local radio show.
14. Have at least three basic programs and pricing packages.
15. Be clear on what you can and cannot provide.
16. Identify thirty to forty referral sources. Become a resource of information for them.
17. Immediately acknowledge a referral.
18. Send creative thank-you gifts to referrals.
19. If you are looking for corporate clients, use Nurture Marketing: www.nurturemarketing.com.
20. Underpromise. Overdeliver.
21. Develop a great logo: www.gologo.com.
22. Use fusion marketing. Identify other companies that have the same kind of target clients and the same standards of excellence that you have.
23. Find targeted mailing lists. Lots of them are available at www.usadata.com.
24. Have an exhibit booth at connected trade shows.
25. Continue contact with your clients. Do ninety-day and six-month checkups.
26. Have an updated website for easy access to information.

27. Send birthday cards, anniversary of coaching success benchmarks, etc.
28. Join three organizations whose members would be ideal clients for you.
29. Have lunch twice a week with someone you can learn from.
30. Write at least one note of encouragement each day to someone.
31. Ask for the order. Be fearless; you've got to close the sale!
32. Get to know the top coaches in your field.
33. Have a personal master mind group or group of advisors.
34. Recognize that 20 percent of your work time in the first year should be spent in marketing.
35. Attend two or three major conferences each year.
36. Read three or four magazines each month. Stay informed for intelligent conversations with your clients. Try *Fast Company*, *Inc.*, *SUCCESS*, and *Entrepreneur*.
37. Have an amazing elevator speech.
38. Use social media to get the word out.
39. Create an audio or video podcast.
40. Write a book.

Simple Business Budget

RBSC Quickie Budget

Item	Monthly Total	Payoff Amount	Behind By
Giving	_____		
Saving			
Bank	_____		
Equipment	_____		
Building	_____		
Building/Wage			
Mortgage	_____	_____	_____
Rent	_____	_____	_____
Repairs/Fees	_____		_____
Storage	_____		_____
Salary Expense	_____		_____
Utilities			
Electricity	_____		_____
Water/Gas	_____		_____
Internet	_____		_____
Phone	_____		_____
Cell Phone	_____		_____
Trash	_____		_____
Food			
Coffee Svc	_____		
Business Meals	_____		
Transportation			
Vehicle	_____	_____	_____
Vehicle 2	_____	_____	_____
Gas/Oil	_____		
Repairs	_____		
Insurance	_____		
Tires	_____		
Shipping	_____		

RBSC Quickie Budget

Item	Monthly Total	Payoff Amount	Behind By
Uniforms	_____		
Benefits			
Disability	_____		
Healthcare	_____		
Life	_____		
Child Care	_____		
Eye Care	_____		
Miscellaneous			
Marketing	_____		
Office Supplies	_____		
Memberships	_____		
Totals:	_____		

Simple Personal Budget

RBSC Quickie Budget

Item	Monthly Total	Payoff Amount	Behind By
Giving	_____		
Saving			
Bank	_____		
Retirement	_____		
College	_____		
Housing			
Mortgage	_____	_____	_____
Second	_____	_____	_____
Repairs/Fees	_____		_____
Rent	_____		_____
HOA Fees	_____		_____
Utilities			
Electricity	_____		_____
Water	_____		_____
Gas	_____		_____
Cable TV	_____		_____
Internet	_____		_____
Phone			
Cell Phone			
Trash	_____		_____
Food			
Groceries	_____		
Eating Out	_____		

RBSC Quickie Budget

Item	Monthly Total	Payoff Amount	Behind By

Transportation

Vehicle	_____	_____	_____
Vehicle 2	_____	_____	_____
Gas/Oil	_____		
Repairs/Tires	_____		
Insurance	_____		
AAA	_____		
Boat Payment	_____		

Clothing _____

Personal

Disability	_____		
Healthcare	_____		
Life	_____		
Child Care	_____		
Eye Care	_____		
Entertainment			

Miscellaneous

Gifts	_____		
Pets	_____		
Memberships	_____		

Totals: _____

Start-Up Checklist

This start-up checklist provides the entrepreneur with a final review prior to launching the business. The form covers prelaunch, start-up, and growth. A thorough review of the details will help you avoid many of the typical mistakes.

Prelaunch Stage

Idea

_____ Brainstorm Your Idea—Think outside the box!

_____ Skill Match/Skills Inventory—What do you do best?

_____ Knowledge Match—What do you know a lot about?

_____ Friends and Family—What do your family/friends think of your idea?

Research

_____ Patent/Trademark—Do you need a patent to protect your product or idea?

_____ Competitor Analysis—Who else does this?

_____ Collect Demographic Data—Who is going to buy this?

_____ Market/Industry Size—Who is your target client?

_____ Regulations—Are there state or federal laws that govern this industry?

_____ Feasibility Planning—Can this make money?

Guidance and Assistance

_____ Visit the Real Business Solution Center—Locate resources, networking, and assistance.

_____ Meet with Advisors—Set an appointment with a business counselor.

_____ Talk to Family and Friends—Seek advice from others.

Idea Testing

_____ Interview—Interview people who know the industry.

_____ Professionals—Line up professionals you might need.

_____ Associations—Seek out any related trade organizations.

_____ Focus Groups—Test your idea and your product at every opportunity.

_____ Prototyping—Do you need to build a working model?

_____ Process Flowcharting—Write down everything that needs to happen before you open.

Financial Planning

_____ Make three- and five-year sales projections.

_____ Project your expenses and cash flow.

_____ Identify sources of funding.

_____ Estimate your expected returns.

_____ Calculate a breakeven and various financial ratios.

Marketing Plan

_____ Develop a detailed sales strategy.

_____ Decide how you will get the word out about your business.

_____ Determine the costs of your promotion and advertising plans.

_____ Determine your financial allocations to marketing, advertising, and promotion.

Business Plan

_____ Develop your road map for success.

Start-up Stage

Register

_____ Choose a business name.

_____ Determine your corporate structure (sole proprietorship, LLC, etc.).

_____ Register your business with the required local, state, and federal agencies.

_____ Apply for any required licenses.

_____ Establish a company bank account.

State

_____ Register with the secretary of state.

County

_____ Determine occupational license and zoning requirements (these vary by city and county).

City

_____ Determine occupational license and zoning requirements (these vary by city and county).

Taxes

_____ Apply for an Employer Identification Number at www.irs.gov.

_____ Register with state sales tax (Department of Revenue).

_____ Consult with a local CPA.

Utilities

_____ Contact utility providers for power, water, Internet, phones, etc.

_____ Obtain liability insurance to cover your business. (Additional policies will be needed to protect fixed and movable assets, professional liability, and environmental liability if applicable.)

Launch

_____ Visit the Real Business Solution Center for individual assistance, on-going training, and support resources.

_____ Protect your financial resources by keeping overhead low and focusing on activities that produce income.

_____ Launch your marketing plan to ensure that clients are aware of your services.

_____ Establish strong financial controls and record keeping.

Growth Stage

_____ Locate sources of funding for growth.

_____ Seek out networking options to expand your market share.

_____ Focus on marketing strategy and message.

_____ Focus on employee acquisition and retention.

_____ Outsource tasks.

_____ Compare leasing versus purchasing of equipment.

_____ Practice efficiency and streamlining techniques.

Contract Templates

FEE-FOR-SERVICE AGREEMENT

(Where you are soliciting work from another company)

This Fee-for-Service Agreement is by and between _____
_____ ("Your Company Name") and
_____ ("Contractor"), and is subject to the terms
and conditions set forth herein below.

ARTICLE I: STATEMENT OF WORK. By entering into this Agreement, the Contractor agrees to perform the scope of work outlined in **Attachment A**.

ARTICLE II: PAYMENT FOR WORK. _(Your Company Name)_ will pay the Contractor for the Work performed, based on the Fee Schedule detailed in **Attachment B**, which is incorporated into and made a part of this Agreement. Total compensation under this agreement shall not exceed $_____, without written agreement of the parties.

ARTICLE III: PAYMENT SCHEDULE. _(Your Company Name)_ shall make payment(s) to the Contractor, for Work performed, within thirty (30) days of receipt of invoice, unless contested by _(Your Company Name)_.

ARTICLE IV: PERIOD OF PERFORMANCE. The performance of this Agreement shall begin on _____, and shall not extend beyond _____, except by written agreement of the parties.

ARTICLE V: TERMINATION. Performance under this Agreement may be terminated by _(Your Company Name) upon _____ days' written notice. The Contractor may terminate performance if circumstances beyond its control preclude continuation of the Work. Upon notice of termination by _(Your Company Name)_, the Contractor will cease Work immediately and will be entitled to be reimbursed for any costs and noncancelable commitments incurred in the performance of the Work, prior to the receipt of notice of termination from _(Your Company Name)_. Reimbursement shall not exceed the total cost specified in Article III, unless provided otherwise by written agreement of the parties.

ARTICLE VI: <u>PROPRIETARY INFORMATION.</u> _(Your Company Name)_recognizes that it may properly hold in confidence information supplied by a Contractor, which _(Your Company Name)_considers essential for the conduct of the Work. Accordingly, _(Your Company Name)_'s acceptance and use of any proprietary information, which may be supplied by the Contractor in the course of the Work, shall be subject to the following:

(a) The information must be marked or designated in writing as proprietary to the Contractor.

(b) _(Your Company Name)_retains the right to refuse to accept any such information.

(c) If _(Your Company Name)_accepts such information as proprietary, it agrees to exercise all reasonable efforts not to reveal the information to others without the permission of the Contractor, unless the information has already been or is subsequently disclosed publicly by third parties, was previously known or subsequently discovered independently by _(Your Company Name)_, without the benefit of the proprietary information, or is required to be disclosed by order of a court of law or other governmental authority. It is agreed that such reasonable efforts by _(Your Company Name)_or other governmental authority will be in lieu of all other obligations or liabilities of _(Your Company Name)_relative to proprietary information.

ARTICLE VII: <u>REPORTS.</u> The Contractor shall furnish _(Your Company Name)_such written reports/results of the Work, at designated times, as may be required by _(Your Company Name)_.

ARTICLE VIII: <u>USE OF NAMES.</u> Neither party will use the name of the other or the name of any of the other's employees in any form of publicity without the written permission of the other. In the case of _(Your Company Name)_, permission of the _____ is required.

ARTICLE IX: <u>ASSIGNMENT.</u> The Contractor may not assign, delegate, or subcontract the duties and obligations of this Agreement without the express, written consent of _(Your Company Name)_. All assignees, delegates, or subcontractors will be bound by the requirements of this Agreement.

ARTICLE X: <u>THIRD-PARTY BENEFICIARY.</u> This Agreement shall inure to the benefit of and be binding upon the parties, their successors, and assigns. No third-party beneficiary rights or benefits whatsoever are expressly or impliedly provided herein.

ARTICLE XI: <u>INDEPENDENT CONTRACTOR.</u> At all times during the performance of the Work that is the subject of this Agreement, the relationship of the Contractor to _(Your Company Name)_ shall be that of independent contractor. Neither the Contractor, nor any officer, employee, nor agent of the Contractor shall be entitled to any benefit of employment by _(Your Company Name)_. Neither party is authorized to act as the agent of the other, nor shall either party be bound by the acts of the other. Contractor and its officers, employees, and agents will adhere to _(Your Company Name)_'s Policies found _____.

ARTICLE XII: <u>NOTICES.</u> Any notices required or permitted by this Agreement shall be in writing and shall be delivered by hand, by facsimile, or by United States mail, postage prepaid to:

_____

_____

_____

_____

ARTICLE XIII: <u>REPRESENTATIONS AND WARRANTIES BY CONTRACTOR.</u> If Contractor is a corporation or a limited liability company, Contractor warrants, represents, covenants, and agrees that it is duly organized, validly existing, and in good standing under the laws of the state of its incorporation or organization and is duly authorized and in good standing to conduct business in the State of _____, that it has all necessary power and has received all necessary approvals to execute and deliver the Agreement, and the individual executing the Agreement on behalf of Contractor has been duly authorized to act for and bind Contractor.

ARTICLE XIV: <u>NO BENEFIT CERTIFICATION.</u> By accepting this agreement, Contractor certifies that no _(Your Company Name)_ employee or official, and no family members of a _(Your Company Name)_ employee or official, will receive a benefit from this _(Your Company Name)_ payment, except as has been previously disclosed, in writing, to _(Your Company Name)_.

ARTICLE XV: <u>TAX CERTIFICATION (APPLICABLE TO AGREEMENTS FOR THE PURCHASE OR LEASE OF TANGIBLE PERSONAL PROPERTY).</u> Contractor certifies that Contractor is appropriately registered to collect and remit sales, use, and lease tax on all taxable sales and leases of personal property in _____ and that Contractor is not barred from bidding for or entering into a contract and that Contractor acknowledges that _(Your Company Name)_ may declare the Agreement void if this certification is false.

ARTICLE XVI: <u>GOVERNING LAW.</u> The Agreement and all of the rights and obligations of the parties hereto and all of the terms and conditions hereof will be construed, interpreted, and applied in accordance with and governed by and enforced under the laws of the State of _____.

ARTICLE XVIII: <u>RESOLUTION OF DISPUTES.</u> The parties agree that any and all claims, controversies of disputes between the parties which arise out of or relate in any way to this Agreement or a breach hereof and which the parties are unable to resolve informally shall be submitted to nonbinding mediation in _____.

ARTICLE XVIIII: <u>LIABILITY.</u> _(Your Company Name)_ and Contractor shall each be responsible for any and all liability resulting from the acts and/or omissions of their respective employees, officers, directors, agents, and contractors. Neither party shall be liable for any liability resulting from the acts and/or omissions of the other party's employees, officers, directors, agents, and contractors.

ARTICLE XX: <u>ENTIRE AGREEMENT MODIFICATIONS.</u> This Agreement supersedes all prior agreements, written or oral, between Contractor and _(Your Company Name)_ and will constitute the entire Agreement and understanding between the parties with respect to the subject matter hereof.

The Agreement and each of its provisions will be binding upon the parties and may not be waived, modified, amended, or altered except by a writing signed by _(Your Company Name)_ and Contractor.

(Your Company Name)

By: _____

Title: _____

Date: _____

CONTRACTOR: _____

By: _____

Title: _____

Date: _____

ATTACHMENT A

SCOPE OF WORK

Note: This section must include a detailed description of the services to be provided.

ATTACHMENT B

FEE SCHEDULE

FEE-FOR-SERVICE AGREEMENT

(Where you are providing product or services for a customer)

This Fee-for-Service Agreement is by and between _____ _____ ("Your Company Name") and _____("Customer"), and is subject to the terms and conditions set forth herein below.

ARTICLE I: STATEMENT OF WORK. _(Your Company Name)_ agrees to use its best efforts to perform the scope of work outlined in **Attachment A**.

ARTICLE II: PERIOD OF PERFORMANCE. The performance of this Agreement shall begin on _____, and shall not extend beyond the estimated completion date of _____, unless by written agreement of the parties. _(Your Company Name)_ shall have no liability to Customer, and shall not be in default if performance is delayed or prevented by any cause beyond _(Your Company Name)_'s control.

ARTICLE III: PAYMENT FOR WORK. The Customer will pay _(Your Company Name)_ for the Work performed, based on the Fee Schedule detailed in **Attachment B**, which is incorporated into and made a part of this Agreement. Total compensation under this Agreement shall not exceed $_____, without written agreement of the parties.

ARTICLE IV: PAYMENT SCHEDULE. The Customer shall make payments to _(Your Company Name)_ on a monthly basis, as invoiced, based upon the Work performed. All payments are due within thirty (30) days of receipt of invoice.

ARTICLE V: TERMINATION. Performance under this Agreement may be terminated by the Customer upon sixty days' written notice. _(Your Company Name)_ may terminate performance if circumstances beyond its control preclude continuation of the Work. Upon termination, _(Your Company Name)_ will be reimbursed for all costs and noncancelable commitments incurred in the performance of the Work, prior to the receipt of notice of termination from the Customer. Reimbursement shall not exceed the total estimated project cost, as specified in Article III, unless provided otherwise by written agreement of the parties.

ARTICLE VI: <u>CUSTOMER PROPRIETARY INFORMATION.</u> _(Your Company Name)_recognizes that it may properly hold in confidence information supplied by a Customer, which customer considers essential for the conduct of the Work. Accordingly, _(Your Company Name)_'s acceptance and use of any proprietary information, which may be supplied by the Customer in the course of the Work, shall be subject to the following:

(a) The information must be marked or designated in writing as proprietary to the Customer.
(b) _(Your Company Name)_retains the right to refuse to accept any such information.
(c) If _(Your Company Name)_accepts such information as proprietary, it agrees to exercise all reasonable efforts not to reveal the information to others without the permission of the Customer, unless the information has already been or is subsequently disclosed publicly by third parties, was previously known or subsequently discovered independently by _(Your Company Name)_, without the benefit of the proprietary information, or is required to be disclosed by order of a court of law or other governmental authority. It is agreed that such reasonable efforts by _(Your Company Name)_ will be in lieu of all other obligations or liabilities of _(Your Company Name)_relative to proprietary information.

ARTICLE VII: <u>REPORTS.</u> _(Your Company Name)_ shall furnish the Customer written reports/results of the Work at designated times, as agreed upon by the parties.

ARTICLE VIII: <u>USE OF NAMES.</u> Neither party will use the name of the other or the name of any of the other's employees in any form of publicity without the written permission of the other. In the case of _(Your Company Name)_, permission of _____ is required.

ARTICLE IX: <u>ASSIGNMENT.</u> Neither this Agreement nor the rights granted to _(Your Company Name)_ by this Agreement shall be assignable or otherwise transferable by _(Your Company Name)_ without the Customer's prior written consent, which shall not be unreasonably withheld. Such assignment shall not relieve _(Your Company Name)_ of its obligations hereunder, and the Customer may ask for reasonable assurances to such effect. Any such assignee of _(Your Company Name)_ shall be bound by the terms stated herein, as if the assignee were the original party to this Agreement.

ARTICLE X: <u>INDEPENDENT CONTRACTOR.</u> The relationship of _(Your Company Name)_ to the Customer shall be that of independent contractor. Neither party is authorized to act as the agent of the other, nor shall either party be bound by the acts of the other.

ARTICLE XI: <u>NOTICES.</u> Any notices required or permitted by this Agreement shall be in writing and shall be delivered by hand, by facsimile, or by United States mail, postage prepaid to:

(Your Company Name)

_____

_____

_____

_____

ARTICLE XII: <u>REPRESENTATIONS AND WARRANTIES BY CUSTOMER.</u> If Customer is a corporation or a limited liability company, Customer warrants, represents, covenants, and agrees that it is duly organized, validly existing, and in good standing under the laws of the state of its incorporation or organization and is duly authorized and in good standing to conduct business in the State of _____, that it has all necessary power and has received all necessary approvals to execute and deliver the Agreement, and the individual executing the Agreement on behalf of Customer has been duly authorized to act for and bind Customer.

ARTICLE XIII: <u>NO BENEFIT CERTIFICATION.</u> By accepting this agreement, Customer certifies that no (Your Company Name) employee or official, and no family members of a _(Your Company Name)_ employee or official, will receive a benefit from this _(Your Company Name)_ payment, except as has been previously disclosed, in writing, to _(Your Company Name)_.

ARTICLE IX: <u>GOVERNING LAW.</u> The Agreement and all of the rights and obligations of the parties hereto and all of the terms and conditions hereof will be construed, interpreted, and applied in accordance with and governed by and enforced under the laws of the State of _____.

ARTICLE X: <u>RESOLUTION OF DISPUTES.</u> The parties agree that any and all claims, controversies of disputes between the parties which arise out of or relate in any way to this Agreement or a breach hereof and which the parties are unable to resolve informally shall be submitted to nonbinding mediation in _____.

ARTICLE XI: <u>LIABILITY.</u> (Your Company Name)_ and Customer shall each be responsible for any and all liability resulting from the acts and/or omissions of their respective employees, officers, directors, agents, and contractors. Neither party shall be liable for any liability resulting from the acts and/ or omissions of the other party's employees, officers, directors, agents, and contractors.

ARTICLE XII: <u>ENTIRE AGREEMENT MODIFICATIONS.</u> This Agreement supersedes all prior agreements, written or oral, between Customer and _(Your Company Name)_ and will constitute the entire Agreement and understanding between the parties with respect to the subject matter hereof. The Agreement and each of its provisions will be binding upon the parties and may not be waived, modified, amended, or altered except by a writing signed by _(Your Company Name)_ and Customer.

(Your Company Name)

By: _____

Title: _____

Date: _____

CONTRACTOR: _____

By: _____

Title: _____

Date: _____

ATTACHMENT A

SCOPE OF WORK

Note: This section must include a detailed description of the services to be provided.

ATTACHMENT B

FEE SCHEDULE

EQUIPMENT/SUPPLIES AGREEMENT

This Agreement is made by and between _(Your Company Name)_ and __
_____ (hereinafter
individually or collectively called "Contractor.")

Section I—Specific Conditions

Equipment and/or Supplies. This Agreement is for _(Your Company
Name)_'s purchase of _____
_____ ("Products"). A complete description of the Products
is set forth in Exhibit A.

Pricing. The pricing for the products is set forth in Exhibit B.

Any price adjustments that are set forth in Exhibit B must be forwarded to
(Your Company Name) no later than ninety (90) days prior to the effective
date of the price adjustment.

Warranties. Warranties covering the products are set forth in Exhibit C.

Effective Date, Term, and Termination. This Agreement shall become effective on _____ and shall remain in effect for
a period of _____, until _____.
Thereafter, the Agreement may be renewed for additional one-year terms
by the mutual written consent of the parties. The Agreement may be terminated, with or without cause, by either party furnishing _____ days'
written notice to the other.

Notices. Notices required under this agreement must be forwarded to the
contacts listed below by registered mail or next-day delivery.

If to (Your Company Name):

_____

_____

_____

_____

If to Contractor:

_____ Contractor Name

_____ Representative

_____ Address and Phone

Section II—General Terms and Conditions

Governing Law. The Agreement and all of the rights and obligations of the parties hereto and all of the terms and conditions hereof will be construed, interpreted, and applied in accordance with and governed by and enforced under the laws of the State of _____.

Resolution of Disputes. The parties agree that any and all claims, controversies of disputes between the parties which arise out of or relate in any way to this Agreement or a breach hereof and which the parties are unable to resolve informally shall be submitted to nonbinding mediation in

_____.

Representations by Contractor. If Contractor is a corporation or a limited liability company, Contractor warrants, represents, covenants, and agrees that it is duly organized, validly existing, and in good standing under the laws of the state of its incorporation or organization and is duly authorized and in good standing to conduct business in the State of _____, that it has all necessary power and has received all necessary approvals to execute and deliver the Agreement, and the individual executing the Agreement on behalf of Contractor has been duly authorized to act for and bind Contractor.

Proprietary and Confidential Information. Contractor acknowledges and agrees that information supplied by _(Your Company Name)_ to Contractor under this agreement that is marked "proprietary" ("Proprietary Information") are proprietary to _(Your Company Name)_. Contractor will hold all Proprietary Information in strict confidence. Accordingly, Contractor's acceptance and use of any Proprietary Information, which may be supplied by _(Your Company Name)_ under this Agreement, shall mean that Contractor agrees not to reveal the Proprietary Information to others without written permission of _(Your Company Name)_, unless the Proprietary Information: (i) has already been disclosed publicly by third parties, who had the right to disclose the information; (ii) is received from a third party without limitation on disclosure; (iii) was previously known or subsequently independently discovered by Contractor without the benefit of the disclosure of the Proprietary Information by _(Your Company Name)_ as evidenced by

200

Contractor's written records; or (iv) is required to be disclosed by order of a court of law or other governmental authority. No express or implied licenses or other rights are provided to Contractor under any patents, patent applications, trade secrets, know how, or other proprietary rights of _(Your Company Name)_. Contractor shall not use any material or other proprietary rights of _(Your Company Name)_ to perform internal research or development, to perform contract research or development, to screen compound libraries, to develop, produce, or manufacture products for sale, or to conduct research activities that result in any sale, lease, license, or transfer of the material or Proprietary Information. Contractor covenants and agrees to not assert any intellectual property rights in the Proprietary Information. The restrictions on use and disclosure of the Proprietary Information shall expire five (5) years after disclosure.

TAX CERTIFICATION

<u>(Applicable to agreements for the purchase or lease of tangible personal property)</u>

By accepting this agreement, Contractor certifies that Contractor is appropriately registered to collect and remit sales, use, and lease tax on all taxable sales and leases of personal property in _____.

Compliance with Laws. Contractor shall observe, perform, and comply with or require compliance with all federal, state, and local laws, ordinances, rules, and regulations and all amendments thereto which in any manner may affect the operation and contractor's activities undertaken pursuant to this agreement. The contractor shall also comply with all state and local building, fire, health, zoning laws, codes and/or regulations that affect or that are applicable to contractor's activities and operations hereunder. The furnishing of materials, supplies, equipment, or services to _(Your Company Name)_ under this purchase order, contract, requests, or construction specification constitutes assurance by the contractor or contractor of his compliance with applicable provisions of and pertinent regulations.

Liability. Each party shall be responsible for any and all liability resulting from the acts and/or omissions of their respective directors, officers, employees, agents, and contractors. Neither party shall be responsible for any liability resulting from the acts and/or omissions of the other party's directors, officers, employees, agents, and contractors.

Contractor Indemnification. The contractor hereby covenants and agrees to indemnify and hold harmless _(Your Company Name)_ and its officers, agents, and employees from and against any and all claims or demands by or on behalf of any person, firm, corporation, or governmental authority, arising out of, attributable to or in connection with the use, occupation, possession, conduct, or management of the contractor concerning the equipment or services performed and rendered hereunder, including, but without limitation, any and all claims for injury or death to persons or damage to property. The contractor also covenants and agrees to hold _(Your Company Name)_ harmless from and against all judgment costs, counsel fees, expense, and liabilities incurred in connection with any such claim and any action or proceeding brought thereon, and in case any action is brought against _(Your Company Name)_ by reason of any such claim, the contractor upon notice from _(Your Company Name)_ will resist and defend such action or proceeding by qualified counsel. However, the provisions of this section shall not apply to any claims arising from the negligent or willfully wrongful acts or omissions of _(Your Company Name)_.

Contractor Insurance. Contractor shall, at its own expense, maintain insurance of such types and in such amounts necessary to cover its activities under this Agreement. Workers' compensation, employer liability, and commercial general liability are required for each Agreement. Other types of insurance are only required if expressly stated by _(Your Company Name)_. Minimum types and amounts of insurance are set forth below:

Type of Insurance:	Minimum Limits of Liability Required:
Workers' Compensation	Statutory Limit – Per State
Employer's Liability	$2 million (each employee, each accident & policy limit)

Commercial General Liability (on a form no more restrictive than Insurance Service Office Form CG 00 01 07 98 or its subsequent revisions):

Each Occurrence	$2 million
Personal and Advertising Injury	$2 million
Products/Completed Operations	$2 million
General Aggregate (Per Location)	$2 million
Including Additional Insured Endorsement CG 2026	
Automobile Liability including Garage-keepers single unit Legal liability if appropriate (all owned, hired and non-owned vehicles)	$2 million each accident-combined

These limits may be accomplished through a combination of primary and excess/umbrella liability policies written on a "follow form" basis or forms no more restrictive than the primary policies. Insurance carrier shall be rated A- or better by A.M. Best. Defense costs should be payable in addition to the policy limits with the exception of Professional Liability and Environmental Impairment Liability if indicated. IF ANY COVERAGE IS PROVIDED ON A CLAIMS MADE FORM, THE COVERAGE MUST BE MAINTAINED FOR A MINIMUM OF THREE (3) YEARS BEYOND THE EXPIRATION OF THIS AGREEMENT.

(Your Company Name), its directors, officers, employees, and agents shall be named as additional insured's on the general and, if applicable, auto liability policies. _(Your Company Name)_, its trustees, officers, employees, and agents shall also be named as additional insured's on any professional liability and environmental impairment liability policies if required, and on the umbrella/excess policy if required to meet the minimum limits set forth above. Policies may include a deductible, but the Contractor will be responsible for payment of that deductible on their own behalf and on behalf of _(Your Company Name)_ as an additional insured.

A Certificate(s) of insurance will be provided to _(Your Company Name)_ at _(Your Company Name)_'s request. The Certificate will evidence all coverage required and specify the terms required as noted below. The Certificate will note the additional insured as required above and will provide for at least thirty (30) days' written notice of cancellation or nonrenewal to _(Your Company Name)_.

No Remuneration Certification. _(Your Company Name)_ employees are not allowed to accept personal gifts or gratuities from contractors as an inducement for _(Your Company Name)_ to enter into the agreement. By accepting this agreement, Contractor certifies that it has not offered or given any _(Your Company Name)_ employee or official or their family members any remuneration, except as has been previously disclosed, in writing, to _(Your Company Name)_.

Payment of Invoices. Invoice reconciliation must be provided within twelve (12) months of invoice date. Contractor must provide the (Your Company name) Accounts Payable department with an itemized, monthly statement requesting resolution within this twelve (12)-month period.

Certification and Signature

I have read all of the general and specific terms and conditions of this agreement and am authorized to sign the contract on behalf of my company.

Your Company Name   Contractor

_____   _____
Accepted By   Accepted By

_____   _____
Printed Name   Printed Name

_____   _____
Title   Title

_____   _____
Date   Date

EXHIBIT A

Equipment and Supplies

Note: This page is for you to write a detailed description of the equipment and supplies covered under the contract.

EXHIBIT B

Pricing and Payment Terms

Standard payment terms are Net 30 days from date of invoice unless otherwise stated. Unless otherwise stated, prices are F.O.B. Destination, Freight Prepaid. Contractor assumes all responsibility for damage in transit. Invoice reconciliation must occur within twelve (12) months of invoice date. Contractor shall not impose payment penalties of any kind, including, but not limited to, late fees, service charges, interest, or placing _(Your Company Name)_ on credit hold.

EXHIBIT C

Warranties

Note: This section Is intended for additional text related to warranties provided by the seller.

www.ingramcontent.com/pod-product-compliance
Lightning Source LLC
Chambersburg PA
CBHW051453170526
45166CB00001B/229